Dinner With A
Goddess

So may it be, my sisters,

that in your many sacred kettles,

from your many precious harvests,

and by your many loving hands,

you come to savor the wild brew

of your lush spirit,

and to know the recipe of its being,

the recipe by which you may taste

your own individual essence

and share it with those you love.

Barbara Hort • November 1999

In gratitude for the gift that runs through her.

Published by Full Court Press, Inc.,
215 River North Drive, Atlanta, Georgia 30328
www.unitygrid.com

Printed by BookMasters, Inc.
Mansfield, Ohio 44905

Printed in the United States of America

First Edition – July 2002
ISBN# 0-9718992-0-7
LCCN# 2002091604

All graphic design, including cover, by DiBona Designs, Alpharetta, Georgia 30004

All photography by Hollis McNully, with the following exceptions: Claude Markarian and Lea Beyrouthy by Andre Markarian; Debbie McCanless by Julie Perillo; Lee Gouss by Stieve; Mary Kay Doherty by Daniel Hollsch; and photographs in the biography sections of the women.

Table of *Contents*

Table of Contents

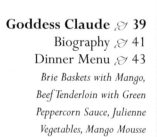

Table of Contents

5

Table of Contents

Table of Contents

The Goddess Within

Call to a new Celestial Earth!

It is time for women to remember

the Goddess Within.

Create the new truth,

step into our divine power

& ancient wisdom,

and reclaim our personal authority.

Patricia DiBona

Mother's Day Goddess Gathering 2001; Top Row—left to right—Sonia Perrine, Jean Perrine
Next Row—Leslie Grove, Kathy Becknell, Sharon O'Connor, Gana Van Laanen, Vickie Lake
Next Row—Sally Vickers, Eve Oliphant, Eleanora Lipton; Bottom Row—Pamela Daniele, Muffet Einwag

Sacred Circle

Welcome to this sacred circle of women. The women of this circle offer you their life stories, their images, and their recipes, with the intention of unveiling the magic in this collaboration by weaving a tapestry greater than any one of us alone could create. As you move through the pages of this book and open your heart to each goddess, you, too will become a part of this circle.

As you explore the pages to come, I invite you to discover different aspects of yourself mirrored in each of the goddesses. As you read about these women who have made a variety of life choices, may you be inspired to embrace more of your own unique expressions. As you discover the wide range of feminine attributes represented by these women, may you acknowledge the miracles of your life and come to see your own journey

as sacred. As this tapestry of goddess energy unfolds, you will come to know that each of us matters, just the way we are.

For the last twenty-five years I have attempted to live my life as if I am an aspect of Divine Consciousness. I have practiced treating all other beings with this same respect. My mission has been honoring the divine essence within each of us. As is the way in all of our lives, I've had moments of great success and moments when I felt a failure. These years have allowed me to know that we are each here for a purpose greater than any of us can imagine. It is this grander sense of life that defines what sacred means to me. When I feel connected to the sacred, I am more sure of myself, more at peace with everyday issues and more confident that my life is divinely directed.

Another way in which I feel connected to the sacred is through the many nurturing friendships I have enjoyed with women over the years. As I've experienced the nuances of how women relate, I have been moved by our natural instincts to embrace others in a circle of care giving and nourishment. I've come to know that when women feel emotionally welcomed and physically safe, they open their hearts instantaneously, embracing all matters of life from a place of inclusion.

Webster defines circle as a 'group of people bound together by common interests; group; coterie.' Encircle means 'to make a circle around; enclose within a circle; surround.' For women, being relational means we seek ways to embrace others who come into our lives. Often we touch that tender place deep within our hearts that moves us to spontaneously include others in a circle of caring, no matter what activity we are doing or whom we encounter. At these moments when we are in that tender heart space, we merge with the flow of divine love, tapping into a healing energy that expands and transforms our lives and the lives of others.

This book honors all women in sacred circle; women making a commitment to participate in a process for the good of all, honoring their commitment by showing as much respect for others as they are able to give themselves. Women gain energy and insights in the company of other women, whether one-on-one or in a group. As women share their personal stories with others, each gains a deeper understanding of her own life's journey. Let our stories unlock your stories, further deepening your appreciation for the beauty in your life.

When we accept another's truth and knowing, our own lives become clearer, truer, healed and more whole. Each woman who has influenced our lives remains with us always. *Dinner With A Goddess* invites you into the center of a sacred circle. Seated all around are these remarkable women who joined with me in the process of creating this book. The geometry of a circle is such

that even if there is only one portion of the circle visible, the rest of the circle is present energetically, allowing the connection to remain whole. As you prepare one goddess's menu in this offering, you are joining the sacred circle created by all the other goddesses.

What makes a woman a goddess? To me, a true goddess is any woman who has the courage to search for ways to make sacred the everyday events of her life. My earliest sense of the spiritual meaning of goddess came from reading *Goddesses in Every Woman* by Jean Shinoda Bolen, MD. Her more recent work *Goddesses in Older Women*, for those of us over fifty, has been equally important for my expanded sense of self. I found greater acceptance of the differences in women by better understanding those goddess aspects that were both familiar and foreign to my natural pattern of expression.

Every woman is a unique combination of mother, daughter, wife, warrior, lover, crone and friend. Our attitudes, preferences, style, choices and passions, all blended with our spiritual philosophies, together weave the fabric of our lives. My way of embracing all women as goddesses has been to create opportunities for all ages to gather in spiritual ritual or social celebrations. *Dinner with a Goddess* is a natural extension of my desire to get beyond judging any woman, thereby tapping into a greater valuing of myself.

Many of the women in the book found it difficult to write their autobiography. As they reflected on their lives, they felt uncomfortable sharing their stories. Few perceived their lives accomplished enough to inspire others. In support of the internal efforts that they faced in writing their stories, I wrote a 'loving reflection' letter to each woman outlining qualities and attributes that I admired, along with moments in their lives that were memorable to me. The following two paragraphs contain the qualities and attributes compiled from the letters to the 'contributing goddesses' in this book.

Accepting, Accomplished, Admirable, Adventuresome, Balanced, Brilliant Capable, Caring, Cautious, Confident, Courageous, Creative, Daring, Dependable, Determined, Dignified, Dramatic, Easy-going, Efficient, Elegant, Expansive, Fair-minded, Fluid, Focused, Friendly, Giving, Gracious, Gregarious, Grounded, Inclusive, Intelligent, Intense, Joyful, Kind, Loving, Loyal, Non-judgmental, Nurturing, Organized, Outrageous, Passionate, Playful, Pragmatic, Precise, Problem-solving, Radiant, Refined, Realistic, Ritualistic, Romantic, Self-contained, Sensual, Sexy, Shy, Smart, Sophisticated, Strong, Supportive, Truthful, Vulnerable.

Likes to have fun. Feels love deeply. Speaks her truth. Shares effortlessly. Thinks clearly. Observes keenly. Keeps her promises. Knows herself. Dares to be different. Strives for balance. Seeks harmony. Creates beauty.

Delights in children. Laughs often. Opens her heart. Is devoted to family. Cherishes her friends. Honors her body. Honors time alone. Handles life straight on. Gives and receives love easily. Supports other women. Is open to new adventures. Seeks truth. Believes in community. Desires to serve humanity. Is committed to a spiritual path. Thinks globally. Never gives up.

As you read these lists, acknowledge which qualities and attributes come easily to you, are natural for you. Then consider which of these aspects seem unfamiliar or unnatural for some reason. What happens to your sense of goddess energy as you say these words out loud to yourself and touch on your feelings of what they mean to you? As I ponder this list of feminine qualities, I see a celebration of the fullness of women's gifts and abilities. I also see a mirror of the powerful qualities that are within all women.

I have always been interested in mentoring women into their fullness. Such mentoring explores questions such as: What allows us as women to embrace our unique qualities, feeling the value of ourselves? What gives us courage? What does it take for each of us to fully accept ourselves just the way we are? I am at a time in my life when these questions invite much inner reflection.

How then do we get so comfortable in our own skin that we feel fully alive? Each woman I know continually searches for her authentic self, that part that doesn't change at different times or around different people; that part that feels deeply and speaks from her place of knowing. I've learned to trust my intuitive knowing. It is a gift that comes from self-calibration and fine-tuning. My experience is that expansion in consciousness is continuous and keeps growing. Each time we make a decision to honor our selves as good enough just the way we are, we are given gifts in consciousness. I am forever aligning with this energy, coming to know it as confident, certain, relaxed and heartfelt. Being with these women in the process of creating this book has shown me how to come to this expansive place more frequently. I am grateful.

My own inner journey of self acceptance fueled my desire to contribute to others out of my own inner passion. I needed a project on which to focus, mentoring myself back into the world. This book became that project. *Dinner with a Goddess* blends my love for intimate friendships with my desire to find a more joyful creative flow in my life. In writing this book, I faced personal challenges that reflected back to me where I could further refine. I feel much of *Dinner With A Goddess* has been divinely orchestrated.

Over the past forty years there have been innumerable books, films, quotes, seminars, lectures, classes and people that have inspired me. Two most recent artistic events I attended in 2001 further shifted my sense of

women and goddess energy. The first was the Annie Leibovitz photography show in Miami Beach called 'Women.' I was surprised at the impact her work had on me, both emotionally and spiritually. Oversized colored images of debutantes hanging next to black and white portraits of badly beaten women; images of Las Vegas show girls before and after makeup; photos of well-known women next to cleaning ladies, waitresses or farmers. I continued to shift with the viewing of each image, feeling the significance of that woman's story within that image.

The other transformational event occurred in the New York Theater, where I saw 'The Vagina Monologues' by Eve Ensler. I had never before been in an audience of 98% women, all ages, by turns laughing and silencing together. I was taken on an emotional journey, every line in the dialogue causing some visceral response.

Both these artistic events were intimate experiences, unlocking energies from deep within. I feel our greatest strength comes from being women, and all we've come to know this to mean.

The final section of this book, describes herbs found in our kitchens that can be made into healing teas. Goddess Cathy has studied herbology since the late 1970's and is the founder of Iris Herbal Products. When Cathy offered to create a list of kitchen herbs that could be made into healing teas, I joyfully said yes. Women have traditionally been responsible for the herb garden, using natural remedies as part of their healing rituals. Women who love to cook like to add herbs to the foods they prepare. Imagine consciously selecting specific herbs to further enhance your meal on the subtle levels, both physically and emotionally. Learn more about Iris Herbal Products by exploring Goddess Cathy's offering in this book.

The purpose of *Dinner With A Goddess* is to celebrate women reclaiming our own spiritual power, our deep sense of sacred self. I invite you to find your own ways of engaging these Goddesses. As you move through the pages of this book, make us a part of your women's sacred circle. Let our photos and personal stories bring you to the realization that your life is every bit as rich a morsel.

Make our recipes your own, adding and subtracting what is needed to get the taste just right, the way you like it. Find ways to deepen the bonds with the women in your life. Divine gifts are embedded in everyday events.

Endless Blessings,
Pamela Daniele

Mother's Day 1956

Here it is a thing that grows,

naturally it is a rose.

But this dainty thing with petals fair

just doesn't seem to quite compare.

I guess you've guessed what I'm trying to say

to complete this day in a special way.

I love you each and every hour,

but still I put it in one flower.

I guess it says in a simple manner,

what all along I've been trying to stammer.

So I'll say it again so you'll be sure to hear,

I love you mom, you are my dear.

Pamela Lynn Bleyle Daniele

Dedication to *My Mother*

It is with great love that I dedicate this book to my mother Eve, the first goddess in my life. In another time and place she would have lived the life of an artist, been a Bohemian, who created from whatever images flowed through her. My earliest memories are of a woman who laughed easily, was relaxed in her lifestyle, had close women friends and gave great parties that always included dancing. Over thirty years ago in California, Eve co-founded Parent's of Adult Schizophrenics, which continues to operate as the name Alliance for the Mentally Ill. Her motivation was to make sense out of my younger brother's journey with schizophrenia. She had to reach deep and pull up much courage. And through all of this, she told her truth and stayed independent.

Eve remains active in her community. She has participated in local theatre for the past fifteen years, both performing and painting the sets. Her first art show was at age 65. She folk danced and tap danced until her knees gave out. Eve continues to give of her time and services through a number of volunteer organizations. At her 80th birthday party more than 200 people showed up from the many diverse areas of her life. And, as is always the way, she was the life of the party. ❦

Eve Oliphant

Creative Team

Patricia DiBona
DiBona Designs
www.dibonadesigns.com

Tapping into her creative flow and priestess energies was divine orchestration. The richness of each page in this book has been blessed with her artist's eye. She committed her spirit (and Daniel Thompson) to this project at a time when it was needed the most. And to make the gift even sweeter, I have a new goddess friend.

Carl McColman
Editorial Consultant
www.carlmccolman.com

After reading his book Aspiring Mystic, I knew I could trust him to help me edit this book. His spiritual perspective on life and deep understanding of goddess energy, gave me the support I needed to successfully complete this offering. Carl's seminar on how to publish a book is where we first met Paul, which led to our meeting Patricia.

20 Contributing Goddesses
The Women Who Said Yes

Where would this project be without each of these women supporting the initial vision for Dinner with a Goddess and staying in the process through the many months of work to complete their contributions? Their gifts of friendship and love nourished newly discovered places within myself during our collaborative journey together. I am forever blessed to know them.

Hollis McNully
Full Court Press, Inc.
www.unitygrid.com

This book would not have taken form without his technical abilities, his photographic artistry and his endless patience with the inner struggles I went through bringing this project to life. Our journey together is rich with the energy of Spirit, expanding our co-creative energies here on earth into our own sacred merging.

Paul Frank
Project Management

I met Paul at a seminar on how to publish a book. Hollis and I were in the right place at the right time, for Paul was the answer to our prayers. The learning curve in publishing a first book is steep and he guided us through this unknown territory with much ease and graciousness. His project management skills made life flow more effortlessly, freeing me to focus elsewhere.

Goddess Isis
Spirit Guide

In my search to find the goddess within, I came upon a list of qualities describing Isis — nurturing, encouraging, supporting though not sustaining, teaching, guiding, showing but not leading. These qualities called to me, weaving together a tapestry of goddess traits I could make my own. I am grateful for all goddess energies that have flowed through me, guiding the creation of this project.

Heartfelt Acknowledgements

Zena Liss Zinger

For the unconditional love given to me for nearly 30 years, inspiring me to keep going and stay true to my spiritual sense of self. She made transition into the heavenly realms in March 2002, giving me gifts of depth and meaning all the way till the end.

Leslie Marks

For the idea to have black and white photos scanned in each goddess biography, deepening the experience of our stories and helping me launch this project.

Lyn Hammond-Gray

For her metaphysical astrological knowing, selecting heavenly aspects under which Dinner With A Goddess *could be born.*

Valued Friendships

For the many friends who have given heartfelt feedback and reassurance during this project and my life—Deva Gouss, Brian Hoey, Leslie Grove, Carlene 'Charlie' Clemons, Sonia Perrine, Colleen Campbell, Kathleen Doherty, Eleanora Lipton, Gana Van Laanen, Alice Grisham, Cindy Gilmore, Mihae Kim, Anne Bleyle and Sheilah Hendrickson.

Divine Orchestration

For all the Beings of Light who have touched my life stream from point of origin to here and now. I am humbled daily and live in gratitude for the many gifts I have been given.

Where's My Soul?

My soul lies hidden in the shadows
Watching while I live my days,
Waiting for the moon again.
Only in stillness will it speak.

I cast out fear and toss my veil
On midnight seas my heart sets sail.
Out there in Eternity
My soul reveals itself to me.

The power for which I stand
Let's me reach out for your hand.

The truth I know is real
Lets me show you how I feel.

This love I give to you
May be the best thing I can do.

Sonia Perrine • January 1998

Annabelle Trettin

Herndon, VA

*Nobody can make you feel
inferior without your consent.*

Eleanor Roosevelt

20

Annabelle Trettin

Favorite red dress
Pleasant Grove, Utah 1956

My brother and me in our western outfits
Pleasant Grove, Utah 1958

Gordon's Studio

On my horse, Paint, holding my trophy won in Western Pleasure Riding Contest – 1960

I was born in Orange, Texas, in 1953. When I was two, my family moved to Pleasant Grove, Utah, where I lived until I was eight. My earliest memories are that I felt carefree and secure. I rode my pony in parades and rodeos, wearing chaps and a belt with my name on it. I played in my favorite red snow suit in winter, looking forward to camping in the summer. School was easy and fun and I especially wanted to learn to read. Reading opened up the world for me, becoming my escape and refuge.

A week after my eighth birthday, my father suddenly died of a heart attack. This altered my life forever. I didn't understand what was happening, just that everything as I knew it changed. We left Utah, moving back to Texas. I went from loving school to hating school, from happy to utterly miserable. The next year we moved to Arkansas, which was home for my mother. My fourth grade teacher was loving and patient, a godsend who provided a safe environment for me to learn again. I wanted to be a fourth grade teacher just like her, setting my path for the future.

Lifeguard – Bridge City, Texas 1971

My first teaching experience was a swim class for children at our family's community pool in Bridge City, Texas. I earned my lifeguard certification, eventually becoming a swim team coach. This was somewhat amazing since I had been so deathly afraid of the water as a child.

I graduated with a B.S. in Education from the University of Arkansas in 1975. I taught for five years in El Paso, Texas. I met my husband Tom in the fall of my first year of teaching. Within two weeks, I knew that he would be my life-long companion. He filled my senses, all those holes and gaps and incompletes that I had felt since I was a little girl.

Tom was career military. As a result, we moved every couple of years, including tours of duty at the U.S. Military Academy at West Point and to Nuremberg, Germany, where I had my first job as a librarian. It was during our time at West Point that I went back to school, earning my Master's Degree in Library Science. I had fabulous libraries at my fingertips, such as Vassar and West Point. For many of my classes, I commuted 2.5 hours each way through Manhattan. Close to the end of my master's program, I grew weary of the commute. My mother offered to come stay with me and keep me company on my commute to and from school. I would not have completed my degree if not for her. I will always be grateful for her loving support.

Wedding Day – El Paso, Texas

Most recent favorite couple shot – June 2001

Our duty assignment after Europe was in the Metropolitan D.C. area, where Tom eventually retired from the military. He is now a consultant in the aerospace industry. In 1993, I got my current job at the U.S. Geological Survey as a cataloger. This specialization is considered one of the most difficult aspects of librarianship. Without an Earth Sciences background, working with research documents in multiple languages has been a tremendous stretch. I am amazed daily that I do this work. The gift of working in the largest science library in the world is that my perspective has totally changed. I now look at Mother Earth not just as the place we live but more from the geological, geophysical, and environmental aspects as well.

Our three-year tour in Germany was one of our best. It was a fabulous experience. I would never have had the opportunity to live, travel and experience Europe as I did. I went into the Czech Republic when it was still an Eastern Block country. I traveled to Budapest, Belgium, Sweden, the Netherlands, Venice and Austria. I believe Austria is one of God's great gifts to the Earth.

Annabelle's Menu

- Veggies and Dip
  in Purple Cabbage Bowl
- Soup Bisque
- Farewell Chicken
- Steamed Asparagus and Wild Rice
- Fruit Pizza
  or
- Peaches and Cream
  Cheesecake

notes:

Dinner with Goddess Annabelle

When I first began entertaining, I thought I had to impress and make the meal extra special (i.e., difficult). What I have learned is that the real treat is just giving my friends an evening away from their own kitchen with a lovingly prepared meal.

I love fresh flowers on the table. I use them in smaller groups, often at each place setting. For this dinner, I would place three to six small vases in the center of the table with a pair of my favorite antique candle-holders that I use both casually and formally. Each stick holds two candles at the same height, so I get the look of flowers and candles without going big and formal.

The table would be set complete with plates, water and wine glasses. When it is time for the meal, I ask everyone to get their plates and serve themselves from the kitchen area, allowing each person a choice of items, as well as portion.

I always have something for a 'beginning'. Since this menu has a rich entrée, soup and a decadent dessert, I would offer a lighter fare of a vegetable platter with dip. One of my favorite presentations for a veggie tray is to hollow out the center of a good-sized purple cabbage, making the cabbage the bowl for the dip and arranging the vegetables in colorful groups around the outside.

Most people love soup. A simple serving idea is to use cups. You know, those smallish china cups with saucers, seasonal mugs to fit the occasion, or whatever you may have. I got this idea from a woman who had a beautiful demitasse cup collection. She prepared soup that could be sipped—no spoon required—and walked around and served soup to her guests in cups from a tray. It's a wonderful way to transition from appetizers to the meal and can easily accommodate a larger group. This soup is one of my favorites.

notes:

Hors d'oeuvres

Ingredients:
- 1 purple cabbage
- fresh pre-cut vegetable selection
- 1 pkg. Knorr's vegetable dip mix
- 1/2 cup light mayo
- 1/2 cup light sour cream

Method:
- Cut off the top 1/3 of the cabbage for a 'lid'. An additional cut off the bottom will allow the cabbage to free stand, if your platter won't accommodate holding it upright.
- For the dip, mix together equal amounts of light mayo, light sour cream and stir in the package of Knorr's vegetable dip mix.

Super Soup Bisque

Ingredients:
- 2 cans of tomato soup
- 2 cans of cream of pea soup
- 4 cans of evaporated milk
- 2 cups of cooked seafood—lobster or shrimp
- 1/3 cup of sherry (drinking or cooking; both work but I prefer drinking)
- 1 individual container of vanilla yogurt
- croutons

Method:
- Heat cans of soup and evaporated milk, stirring to prevent scalding.
- Add about 2 cups of cooked seafood.
- Add sherry to taste.
- Before serving, heat again and add more sherry if desired. Float a dab of yogurt and small croutons on top. (If serving in cups, I omit the croutons.) Serves 8 and can easily be doubled or tripled.

Ingredients:
- 6 boneless chicken breasts,
  1 per person
- 3–4 eggs, well beaten
- 1–2 cups fine breadcrumbs
- 1/2 cup butter
- 1 pkg. fresh mushrooms
- 8 ounces Muenster cheese slices
- 1/2 cup rich chicken broth
- 1 lemon

Method:
- Cut chicken breasts into bite size pieces.
  Cover with beaten eggs. Place in covered
  dish. Refrigerate overnight.
- Pre-heat oven to 350°.
- Using slotted spoon, drop meat into
  crumbs, making sure they get completely
  covered.
- Sauté in butter until lightly browned.
- Put into the casserole-baking dish from
  which you are going to serve.
  Cover with thinly sliced mushrooms, then
  cheese slices.
- Squeeze lemon juice over all.
  Add 1/2 cup of broth.
- Bake 30 minutes.

notes:

Farewell Chicken

This chicken recipe was nameless when I got it. In the military, the commander's house is usually a place where you are invited many times during the course of your tour. We had one duty station where the commander's wife was not comfortable entertaining. You were invited twice only, to a wives luncheon when you arrived and to a farewell dinner with your spouse three years later when you left.

Always serving the same two menus for these occasions, she was very reluctant to share. When we were leaving, I asked for the main dinner recipe. After several requests, I finally showed up on her doorstep unannounced. I promised not to share her recipe with those remaining behind. Sweet persistence prevailed!

I named it 'Farewell Chicken' in honor of the occasion and to the amusement of the women who were leaving. After getting the recipe, I understood why this was her 'old faithful'—assemble ahead of time, only a few ingredients, and fabulous taste, making this a wonderful entrée. I am happy to share.

This dish can be assembled early in the day—up to the point of adding the lemon juice and chicken broth—and then kept in the refrigerator. Or, if you want more zing, add the lemon juice at the time of assembly before putting it into the refrigerator. Try both ways to see which taste you prefer.

Steamed Asparagus and Wild Rice

With emphasis on the entrée and dessert, I keep the sides simple. Steamed asparagus and wild rice would be my first choice. Follow the instructions on the rice package for cooking and quantity.

Desserts

When entertaining friends, I always have a dessert with coffee after dinner. To me it is a lovely way to begin to bring the evening to closure. I allow time in between dinner and dessert. I think dessert tastes better, and is better received, if not rushed. Dessert may be something simple or, more often than not in my home, is rich and decadent. Having friends over is a special celebration.

Peaches & Cream Cheesecake (Winter favorite)

First set of Ingredients:
- 3/4 cup all-purpose flour
- 1 teaspoon baking powder
- 1/2 teaspoon salt
- 1 small pkg. vanilla pudding (not instant)
- 3 tablespoons butter
- 1 egg
- 1/2 cup milk

Second set of Ingredients:
- 8 ounces softened cream cheese
- 1/2 cup sugar
- 3 tablespoons of juice from canned peaches

- (1) 15–20 ounce can sliced peaches, drained well

Method:
- Pre-heat oven to 350°.
- Combine first set of ingredients and mix for two minutes. Pour into a pie plate that has been lightly sprayed with Pam.
- Combine second set of ingredients.
- Fold peaches into this mixture.
- Spoon onto batter within half inch of edge of pan.
- Sprinkle cinnamon on top and bake for 35 minutes. Make sure crust is golden brown.
- Let cool and refrigerate.
  Serve at room temperature.

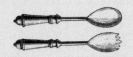

Fruit Pizza (Summer favorite)

This is easy and looks so cool and refreshing.

Ingredients:
- 1 roll Pillsbury sugar cookie dough
- 1 cup orange juice
- 8 ounces cream cheese—pineapple or strawberry flavored
- 2/3 cup sugar
- 2 tablespoons cornstarch
- 1/2 teaspoon salt
- fresh fruit—bananas, strawberries, kiwis, blueberries, mandarin oranges

Method:
- Pre-heat oven to 350°.
- Slice different kinds of fresh fruit to make the toppings, i.e., kiwi, bananas, strawberries, blueberries, mandarin oranges, etc. Set aside.
- Line a round pizza pan with foil.
- Press Pillsbury sugar cookie dough into the pan and bake for 12 minutes. Let cool. Make sure the dough is well baked to prevent sogginess once the fruit is added.
- Spread the cookie dough with soft cream cheese—pineapple or strawberry flavored.
- Lift the cookie out of the pan, peel off the foil and place the cookie on a serving plate.
- Arrange the fruit decoratively on the cookie.

Method to Prepare the Orange Glaze:
- Mix sugar, cornstarch, salt and orange juice together. Boil one minute.
- Cool five minutes before pouring over the 'pizza'.
- Refrigerate before serving.

Each person has her own safe place
—running, painting, swimming,
fishing, weaving, gardening.
The activity itself is less important
than the act of drawing on your own resources.

Barbara Gordon

Cathy Hope

Questa, NM

The best mind-
altering drug is truth.

Lily Tomlin

Cathy Hope

Produce Manager— Atlanta, Georgia 1982

Organic Gardener – Questa, New Mexico 1991

Potter – Appalachia, Virginia 1973

I was born in Lakewood, Ohio, in 1951. My early childhood was spent in Cleveland before moving to York, Pennsylvania, where I lived until I was 18. I completed an alternative college program before starting a series of careers in different states. I was a potter in Appalachia, Virginia, for six years. I moved to Atlanta in 1977, becoming a produce buyer for a natural foods cooperative. My next four-year career was spent as an organic landscaper. While still in Atlanta I studied herbs, focusing first on flower essences and then on aromatherapy. I created Iris Herbal Products in 1982.

When I moved to northern New Mexico in October of 1988, much of what I understood about both the world in general and herbs in particular altered dramatically. My offerings in Iris Herbal Products expanded to tinctures in 1994 and supplements in 1998. Now I see myself primarily as a 'health coach' and a maker of herbal remedies. I work with folks to maximize their healing potential through the synergy of diet, lifestyle, herbs and nutritional supplements. I do not diagnose or prescribe, but rather work with a person's self or a doctor-diagnosed condition. I then dive into my extensive research library, putting together a comprehensive health enhancement plan.

Moving to New Mexico caused me to re-learn how to garden. I changed climate, altitude, and USDA zone. Because I'd been gardening since I was ten and

Finished passive solar greenhouse – Questa, New Mexico 2001

Building passive solar greenhouse—
Questa, New Mexico 1999

professionally landscaping since my 30's, this was a huge learning curve. I am grateful that all my experimenting led me to better understand semi-arid gardening. Using permaculture precepts has proven especially successful. In 1999, I designed a completely passive and active solar greenhouse, receiving a small USDA grant to do organic research. With the help of friends, I constructed this design using natural materials for insulation and rain-

water as a water supply. Finally, I can grow a ripe bell pepper anytime of the year, in any kind of weather.

Another way I feel joy is experiencing moments in some new place in nature, like in the wild or in a cultivated garden, preferably with a friend. There was one of those moments when a friend and I went on a nature stroll in late June in a river canyon in Northern New Mexico. It took us over three hours to walk two miles because we had to look up every flower we saw but didn't recognize, commenting on its shape, size, aroma, or other salient characteristics. We laughed at how pokey we were, realizing the gift we shared in the knowing caused no need to rush.

Besides nature strolling and gardening, my favorite hobby is reading. At 18, I decided TV didn't hold much interest and neither did going to movies. I am also not a big party person. Reading became my major entertainment and relaxation. Periodically, I feel compelled to explore some specific topic, immersing myself in non-fiction. Otherwise, I read a wide variety of novels, including science fiction, fantasy, contemporary/magic realism and mysteries.

My life-long spiritual path has been about under-standing 'who I am', becoming myself more fully and more truly no matter what might happen or where the journey might lead. When I was younger, my drive for integrity and the challenges of being authentic had dire consequences, bringing hard times and much soul searching. My life has reached a more mellow and balanced flow, with these qualities of high integrity and authenticity playing out in my daily life choices like how I earn my living, what I eat, where I spend my money, and how I participate in my local community. Yet, sometimes the challenge is still to accept myself just as I am even with my perceived imperfections. When I make mistakes, I practice not focusing so much on fear and doubt, or whatever I think could be better, but rather focusing on the perfection of the moment just the way it is.

I am currently exploring two spiritual principles – 'One Day at a Time' and 'Tell the Truth.' One day at a time is often tricky because I live alone with my dog Rhubarb, am self-employed, work a large garden, and participate in local politics and environmental concerns, all of which take time and energy. I can easily feel overwhelmed. I made a few resolutions this year to bring greater balance into my life, dedicating one day every week for rest and relaxation, as well as scheduling some time for a real vacation, even if only for a few days to visit with friends. So I'm doing my best, one day at a time, letting go of my tendencies to give myself a hard time about what is left on my list at the end of each day.

And then there is my commitment to tell the truth. Back in the late seventies, when I first became a feminist, I read Adrienne Rich's essay, *Women and Honor: Some Notes on Lying*. I knew right then that this was going to be a life-long process of learning how to perceive what is true for me, how to acknowledge it to myself, and then find the courage to tell what is true for me without judgment of others.

Working on this cookbook has been an expansive experience. Sharing what we love doubles the pleasure. May you, the reader, find a new herb, flower, or 'weed' to add to your culinary repertoire.

Cathy Hope

Iris Herbal Products Office – Questa, New Mexico 2001

You can contact Cathy at:
www.irisherbal.com or
www.passivesolargreenhouse.com.

Cathy's Menu

- Wild Fruit Bread
- Wild Asparagus Frittata
- Herb and Flower Salad
  - Early Spring Salad
  - Mid-Spring Salad
  - Summer Salad
  - Autumn Salad
- Herbal Sun Tea
  - Spring Mint Tea
  - Summer Lemon Cooler
    or
- Rose Hip Tea

notes:

Dinner with Goddess Cathy

Ever since I was a little girl, I've loved to see, touch, smell and grow flowers. To me flowers, herbs and food plants are all just different members of the same huge, loving extended family. Some of them nourish our physical bodies; some of them can heal various ailments; some change our consciousness; and some are turned into clothing, even coloring that cloth.

I've been an herbalist for over 20 years. Herbs, flowers and even weeds show up regularly in my meals. I've approached my menu idea using 'wild foods' as basic ingredients. Elsewhere in the book is a compilation of herbs and spices found in most well-stocked kitchens, and the common ailments they are useful for treating.

Today, many people think our Western technological civilization is humanity's greatest achievement. Still, let us not forget how far we've come because of the countless generations of humans interacting with the plant realm to determine which plants were food, which were poison, which were medicine, which plants could be used for dye or clothing or building materials, and which plants could be used to make cordage (cording or rope). This long exploration and oral tradition is the miracle that brings gifts to all of us humans in our daily lives.

Because many of the ingredients are 'wild', it would be a good idea to check in your local library or bookstore for books on plant identification, so you don't pick the wrong plant. Or maybe you know a local herbalist who can guide you, or take you on an herb walk.

Wild Fruit Bread

Ingredients:
- 1 cup mashed pawpaw, wild persimmons, wild apricots, wild strawberries or very ripe bananas
- 5 1/2 tablespoons unsalted butter (organic is really best)
- 2/3 cup Sucanet (alternative sweetener)
- 2 large farm eggs or organic eggs, lightly beaten,
- 1 teaspoon vanilla extract
- 1 1/3 cups unbleached white flour (or 1/2 whole wheat and 1/2 white)
- 1/2 teaspoon dried orange rind, or 1 teaspoon fresh orange zest
- 1/4 teaspoon salt
- 1/2 teaspoon baking soda
- 1/4 teaspoon baking powder
- 1/2 cups coarsely chopped pecans or walnuts

Have all ingredients at room temperature.

Method:
- Pre-heat the oven to 350°.
- Oil an 8 1/2 X 4 1/2 inch (six cups) loaf pan.
- Whisk the dry ingredients together thoroughly.
- In a large bowl, beat together butter, eggs, vanilla, and Sucanet two to three minutes until lightened in texture and color.
- Add flour mixture slowly until blended.
- Fold in the fruit and nuts until just combined.
- Scrape the batter into the pan and spread evenly.
- Bake 50 to 60 minutes, until a toothpick inserted in the center comes out clean. Let cool on a rack for a few minutes before taking out of the pan.

Wild Asparagus Frittata for Four

Ingredients:
- 2 tablespoons olive oil
- 1/2 cup wild onions or regular onions, thinly sliced
- 1/2 cup wild mushrooms or regular mushrooms
- 3/4 cup wild asparagus tips or regular asparagus tips
- 5 large farm eggs, or organic eggs
- 1/2 teaspoon salt and a pinch of black pepper
- 1/2 cup grated Parmesan cheese
- 3 tablespoons minced fresh parsley
- 1 tablespoon organic butter

Method:
- Heat 1 tablespoon olive oil in a large skillet over medium heat.
- Add wild onions and cook until soft, stirring frequently.
- Add mushrooms, stirring until soft. Transfer vegetables to a strainer and let cool completely.
- Lightly steam asparagus tips and add to strainer to cool.
- Pre-heat broiler.
- Beat eggs until smooth, adding salt and a pinch of black pepper.
- Add the cooled asparagus, onion and mushroom mixture to the eggs, along with Parmesan cheese and minced parsley.
- Heat butter and remaining olive oil in a large skillet over medium heat. When hot, pour in egg mixture.
- Reduce heat and cook until bottom is set, then place under the broiler for 60 seconds to finish cooking the top.
- Loosen the frittata with a spatula and slide it onto a plate, or just cut into quarters and place on each person's plate.

Herb and Flower Salad

Early Spring Salad

Ingredients:
- 1 cup baby lettuce or baby spinach leaves
- 1 cup day lily shoots
- 1 cup chickweed
- 1 cup young dandelion leaves
- 1/4 cup curly dock leaves
- 1/4 cup redbud flowers (or chives)

Method:
- Chop all ingredients together and serve with vinaigrette dressing.

notes:

Mid-Spring Salad

Ingredients:
- 1/2 cup cattail shoots
- 1 cup violet leaves and flowers
- 1 cup orach leaves (red and/or green)
- 1/2 cup red or white clover flowers

Method:
- Chop all ingredients together and serve with vinaigrette dressing.

Summer Salad

Ingredients:
- 1 cup baby beet, kale and/or lettuce and spinach leaves
- 1 cup purslane
- 1/2 cup lamb's quarters
- 1/2 cup wood sorrel (or lemon balm and salad burnett leaves)
- 1/2 cup mixed flowers (calendula, nasturtium, chamomile, mint, comfrey, borage, roses, bee balm, evening primrose or holly hocks)

Method:
- Chop all ingredients together and serve with vinaigrette dressing.

Autumn Salad

Ingredients:
- 1 1/2 cups chickweed
- 1 cup common mallow leaves
- 1 cup wild or commercial watercress
- 1 1/2 cup grated Jerusalem artichokes

Method:
- Chop all ingredients together and serve with vinaigrette dressing.

Herbal Sun Tea

Spring Mint

Ingredients:
- 5 ounces fresh young mint leaves
- 1 ounce fresh young catnip leaves
- 1 ounce fresh red and/or white clover blossoms
- 1 ounce fresh violet leaves and flowers

notes:

Summer Lemon Cooler

Ingredients:
- 3 ounces fresh lemon balm leaves (and flowers)
- 3 ounces fresh mint leaves (and flowers)
- 1 ounce fresh borage flowers (and/or calendula, chamomile, comfrey, mullein)
- 1 ounce fresh rose petals

Method for both Herbal Teas:
- Pick herbs and flowers between 8:00 AM and 10:30 AM, and place into a clean half-gallon glass jar.
- Add 64 ounces of cool water. Cover and set in the sun for two to four hours. The amount of time depends on how hot the sun is and how strong you want your tea.
- Strain and chill, drinking within two to three days.

Sun Tea can also be made on a cloudy day by heating the water first and letting the tea sit for a few hours.

Fall Rose Hip Tea

Ingredients:
- 2 ounces fresh rose hips per 8 ounces of water
- honey and lemon to taste

Method:
- Chop up fresh rose hips.
- Bring water to a boil.
- Put rose hips in a teapot; add water, cover and let sit for ten minutes.

One is not born a woman,

one becomes one.

Simone De Beauvoir

Claude Markarian

Alpharetta, GA

*We grow neither better nor
worse as we get old,
but more like ourselves.*

Mary Lamberton Becker

Claude Markarian

5 years old, 1963

18 years old, 1976

Myself at 22, 1980

I was born and raised in Beirut, Lebanon. I found the love of my life while a student in Paris, France, some 25 years ago. Mark and I are together to this day. We have two sons who are the center of our lives. The days they were born were two of my most joyful moments, despite the ugly war that was going on around us, forcing us out of our country.

And, something good comes out of every ordeal: It made us realize that nothing was more precious than life, strengthening our family bond. It gave us the ability to turn tragedy into happiness, despair into hope, ordeal into challenge.

Once in the U.S. I took an interest in my parent's business, after discovering the beautiful and exciting world of gems. I decided to become a gemologist to help out at their jewelry store. I love being surrounded by beauty, and gemstones can be quite fascinating.

Cedars of Lebanon, 1996

Beit-eddine Palace, Lebanon, 1996

One of my main hobbies, and most enjoyable activities other than traveling and reading, is cooking. While still back home in Lebanon, I belonged to a gourmet club taught by one of the finest French chefs. This gave me the opportunity to improve my gourmet skills and acquire a passion for entertaining.

My beautiful family
Front row: Standing, son Andre
Second row: Playing peek-a-boo, son Patrick
Back row: Me and my husband, Mark

I try to collect recipes from all over the world. Every trip I take adds something new to my repertoire, a new ingredient, or a garnish, or food combination. I owe a lot to my dear husband who tastes every dish, giving me his unbiased opinion and endless encouragement and support.

I enjoyed being part of this project. Each contribution reflects its owner's creativity and imagination. It gives me a sense of accomplishment. I feel it's all about sharing and consider my participation to be a very rewarding experience.

Claude

Dinner with Goddess Claude

Whether you are planning an elegant dinner party or a special occasion family dinner, this menu is sure to delight your guests. It will also surprise you with your new culinary skills and imagination. It combines the best of fancy and exotic recipes, giving it an extra festive flair.

Putting a menu together for the perfect, unforgettable dinner experience is a real work of art: creating contrasts in flavors, colors and textures can be fun and challenging. Foods should complement each other; for example, serving a bland food with a full-flavored sauce, or presenting a light, refreshing dessert after a heavy meal.

I personally enjoy thinking and writing about food almost as much as cooking it. I have the most fun trying to reconstruct at home a delicious dish eaten at a restaurant. I love sharing new recipes with family and friends, who always seem pleased to taste the results of my cooking adventures.

There are no limits to where your imagination and creativity can take you. Remember, you are creating a picture at the dinner table with the table-setting and the food. Make sure to give it your personal touch, like adding an attractive garnish, enhancing the total effect and turning a plain food into something special. After all, savoring a delicious meal is an adventure to the mind and a delight to the senses.

Claude's Menu

- Brie Baskets with Mango
- Beef Tenderloin
  with Green Peppercorn Sauce
- Julienne Vegetables
- Mango Mousse

notes:

Brie Baskets with Mango

Ingredients:
- 8 ounce package of Phyllo Dough
- 1 large ripe mango
- 10 ounces Brie cheese
- vegetable oil spray
- 2 tablespoons sliced almonds
- 2 tablespoons brown sugar
- 6 hole muffin pan

Method:
- Pre-heat oven to 350°.
- Peel and slice mango. Set aside.
- Roughly remove white skin from Brie and cut into small strips.
- Spray muffin mold with vegetable oil
- Cut 18, 6" Phyllo Dough squares.
- Lay 1 square in bottom of mold, shaping it with hand to form a nest. Spray lightly with oil. Lay another square on top of the first one, spray with oil, and finally a third square. Repeat this layering procedure for all 6 holes.
- Bake until golden brown.

- Pre-heat oven to 375°.
- Shortly before serving, fill browned baskets up with alternating cheese and mango, starting with Brie on the bottom.
- Sprinkle top with brown sugar and sliced almond to taste. Bake for 12–15 minutes. Cheese should be soft but not completely melted.

Suggestions:
- Serve with your choice of fruit and nut chutney on the side. More than three squares of dough can be used for each basket.
- Empty dough baskets can be made in advance. Just fill them up and finish baking them right before serving.

Beef Tenderloin with Green Peppercorn Sauce

Ingredients:
- 1 whole four-pound beef tenderloin, peeled and trimmed
- 1 tablespoon vegetable oil
- 1 stick of butter (4 ounces)
- 3 tablespoons green peppercorns
- 1/3 cup Cognac
- 1/3 cup port
- 8 ounces sour cream
- parsley for garnish

Method:
- Pre-heat oven to 400°.
- Coarsely crack the peppercorns with mortar and pestle. Mix in 3/4 of the butter stick. Coat all sides of the beef with this creamy mixture.
- Heat a pan or pot (large enough to contain the meat) adding the 1 tablespoon of oil and the remaining 1/4 stick butter. Sear beef on all sides on high heat until well browned.
- Add Cognac and port and carefully flambé. Reduce heat to medium setting and let cook for 10 minutes.
- Transfer roast to a heated ovenproof dish and continue cooking in preheated oven to desired doneness: meat thermometer should read 135° for a rare center, or approximately 30–35 minutes for medium rare.
- Just before serving, add sour cream to pan juices (meat juices, port and Cognac), stir well, add salt to taste.
- When tenderloin is done, transfer to serving platter and cover with the sauce. Slice according to your guests' preferences, serving the roast ends to those who prefer it medium to well done. Garnish with snipped parsley.

Suggestions:
- Steps including searing the beef can be made up to two hours ahead of time.
- Do not let the cream sauce boil too much, it will separate. If so, to obtain a smooth, creamy sauce, add I teaspoon corn flour, diluted in I tablespoon cold water, while continuously stirring.

Julienne Vegetables

Ingredients:
- 1/4 cup butter
- 1 onion, finely chopped
- 1 clove garlic, crushed
- 2 large zucchinis
- 4 large carrots
- garlic salt, black pepper
- chopped fresh parsley or chives for garnish

Method:
- Wash and trim zucchinis and cut into thin strips. Peel carrots and cut into thin strips. Set aside.
- Melt the butter in a skillet and fry the onion until soft. Mix in garlic.
- Add vegetables and stir-fry for 5 minutes. Vegetables should remain a little crunchy. Because carrots take a longer time to cook than zucchini, you might want to steam them in the microwave for 4–5 minutes before stir-frying them.
- Season with garlic salt and pepper to taste.
- Garnish with chopped fresh parsley or chives.

Mango Mousse

Ingredients:
- 2 large ripe mangoes (about I pound)
- 1 large mango for decoration
- 1 envelope unflavored gelatin (1/4 ounce)
- 1/4 cup lemon juice
- 1/2 cup sugar
- 1/2 cup heavy whipping cream
- 1 teaspoon vanilla sugar or 1 teaspoon vanilla extract
- 2 egg whites
- fancy shaped mold

Method:
- Peel and pit mangos. Blend in mixer with sugar.
- In a small saucepan, sprinkle gelatin over the lemon juice. Stir over low heat until gelatin is completely dissolved.
- Add vanilla extract and mix with the mango purée for a few seconds.
- Pour into a bowl and refrigerate for 10 minutes.
- Meanwhile, whip the cream until it forms soft peaks.
- Whip the egg whites with a pinch of salt and the vanilla sugar until firm.
- Carefully incorporate egg whites and whipping cream to the chilled mango purée.
- Rinse inside of mold with cold water, drain but do not dry.
- Fill it up with the mango mousse.
- Refrigerate at least 4 hours.
- Just before serving, peel one mango, then slice it into thin slices.
- Dip mold briefly in warm water to loosen edges of mousse. Un-mold onto a serving platter.
- Garnish with mango slices.

This dessert can be made completely the day before. Just un-mold and decorate before serving .

I'll not listen to reason.

Reason always means what

someone else has got to say.

Elizabeth Gaskell

Debbie McCanless

Atlanta, GA

Don't compromise yourself.
You are all you've got.

Janis Joplin

Debbie McCanless

Me and my precious Boo (Sugar) about
a year before she left this world, 1997.

Getting ready for our first trip to 4-H camp.
I'm 10, Sugar is about 4, 1979.

My life has been wrapped in a blanket of art, animals and good friends. I was creative from the time I could think and found media for my expression from the world around me. My scholastic life was centered on my artistic expressions as well. Having had a very advanced learning experience in kindergarten, I was more than prepared for my elementary school life. I was often asked to do art projects for the teachers while my counterparts did school work. My love for art would take me all the way to the University of Georgia, where my love for visual art melded into a great love for its history. This became my major study and major love during those years.

I learned a love for animals at birth from my mother. We always had a cat, a dog or two and I even showed Old English Sheepdogs when I was quite young. The absolute love of my life came in the form of a beautiful copper Quarter Horse named Sugar. I got Sugar when I was seven years old and she was one. I trained her myself, or should I say we trained each other. This was hands down the most amazing time of my life to date. Only someone who has been there can truly understand the feeling of the bond created with such a magnificent creature. I lost Sugar about three years ago, and have struggled daily to replace the empty space she left in my heart. I have not yet succeeded.

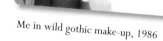

Do we look like a bad rock band? Me, with my two soul mates, Phillip McCanless and Gina Sandler, 1986

This was my young life. I never got into trouble and never got into fads or fashion. I just wanted to see my horse first thing in the morning and last thing at night. My mom, having had horses all her life as well, was my best friend and we spent every day riding and playing. I would go back to that time without a thought. In my eyes, this was the perfect childhood.

As I got older, I began realizing the importance of my peers. I never was into cliques in high school and was never too concerned about what people thought of me. The close friends I did make in high school continue to be true friends. At 16, I started working at a movie theatre. What a wonderful job to have as a kid, free movies and late nights with your friends. I highly recommend it. The friends I made at the theater are also still in my life, and I appreciate their continuing roles in my life. This is most

Me in wild gothic make-up, 1986

especially true of my soul mates, whom I will always love. Those relationships taught me so much about life, especially about myself.

I have since added quite a large diverse group into my mix of friends. They challenge my life both mentally and physically. I have experienced through these friends both total elation and complete sadness. I have learned and grown so much. My mother and father divorced when I was young, and I have always felt a great challenge identifying with the males in my life. Even

Prized possessions – 1995 Triumph Thunderbird and 1995 Harley Low Rider.

with this, I have managed to surround myself with men as both friends and roommates, with very little female influence in my world. I have learned a great deal about the conflicts that can erupt between the sexes. We are very different creatures.

I am now learning about life through the eyes of the women around me. I was very excited about the possibility of contributing to a body of work totally comprised of the thoughts and ideas of other women. This cookbook came at a very pivotal and important time in my life. I have changed so drastically in the past couple of years. I've discovered this change to be maturity.

I find pleasure in working on and creatively modernizing my 60-year-old house. I like working in the yard and watching my plants grow. I ride and collect motorcycles.

I like playing with, and laughing at, the most wonderful Great Dane dog in the world. Most importantly, I am discovering the contentment I find in loving things once ignored that now make up my life. I have a great new love who has taught me the importance of the simple things in life and I revel in them everyday.

My main hope for the future: To have the opportunity to experience the world from the seat of a motorcycle, while continuing to learn who I am. I am working on this vision right now.

Me and my girl on the 1976 Goldwing. Riding around Chattanooga, Trail of Tears ride, 2000.

Debbie's Menu

- Hommus on Tandoori Nan
- Spinach Salad with Fried Tofu
- Thai Peanut Sauce Dressing
- White Wine
- Bananas Foster

notes:

Dinner with Goddess Debbie

I am a vegetarian. I have chosen two favorite dishes as my offering for the Goddess cookbook. This meal is a perfect Sunday 'deck' dinner, or lunch or brunch…whatever.

I call it fusion cuisine. It is a melding of Middle Eastern and Thai. My idea of the perfect meal is one in which I can go from start to table in about 30 minutes with minimum hassles.

This meal is very good served with a nice, not too dry, white wine. I recommend Bridlewood Chenin Blanc. I hope you will have a few people over to enjoy a day in the sun and this nice summer meal.

The Perfect Hommus

You will need either a food processor or a blender. I find I can get a better consistency with the food processor. I like it VERY smooth.

Ingredients:
- 2 cans Goya chick peas
  (Goya gives the best flavor)
- 4 to 5 cloves of garlic. Go crazy, you can never use too much garlic!
- 1 lemon or about 3 tablespoons lemon juice
- 3 tablespoons olive oil
- 3 tablespoons Tahini
- 1 tablespoon black pepper (to taste)
- 2 tablespoons crushed red pepper
- pinch of salt

Method:
- In food processor/blender blend all ingredients. It is important, for consistency, to use one can of chick peas drained and one including the juice. Blend to death. As far as spices go, I usually like a bit more crushed red pepper, which adds a great spicy 'zing'.

- Add the black pepper, crushed red pepper and salt at the end of the blending process. Adjust the spices in your final creation to fit your taste buds.

notes:

notes:

This hommus tastes best when it is at room temperature with a drizzle of olive oil around the edge and a little paprika sprinkled on top.

It is also best served with toasted Tandoori Nan instead of the traditional pita bread. You can find Nan at most farmer's markets. It's worth the effort to find Nan because it really makes all the difference.

I also like to add a side bowl of pepperoncinis. Try this…a bite of hommus on Nan… then a bite of pepperoncini.

…mmmmmmm.

Spinach Salad with Fried Tofu and Thai Peanut Sauce Dressing

Peanut Sauce Dressing

Ingredients:
- 1/4 cup fresh ginger, finely chopped
- 5 cloves garlic
- I cup peanut butter
  (all natural crunch is best)
- 1 tablespoon cayenne pepper
- 2 tablespoons cilantro, freshly chopped
- 2 tablespoons honey
- 1/2 cup apple cider vinegar
- 1/8 cup water

Method:
- Add all ingredients and blend together. You want a nice spicy peanut/ginger taste with a hint of vinegar, cilantro and garlic.
- It is always good to let the mixture sit for a while to help blend all the flavors. Blending all these ingredients together will give you taste and texture.
- I generally will add more cayenne, cilantro and ginger once I have blended everything.
- If you want more of a dressing consistency, add water or vinegar.

I usually enjoy serving this dressing in a small bowl on the side, where each guest can decide whether to use it as a dip or pour it on as a dressing.

Fried Tofu

Tofu Batter Ingredients:
- 1 or 2 packages extra firm tofu
- 1 cup flour
- 1/2 cup cornstarch
- 1 tablespoon pepper
- pinch of salt
- 2 eggs or carton of Egg Beaters
- 1 cup breadcrumbs
- 1 tablespoon crushed red pepper
- vegetable oil in a Fry Daddy, or deep pan

Method:
- Tofu fries best when it has been depleted of as much water as possible. I found it is good to put it in a colander and weight it down with several heavy bowls. Leave it for 30 minutes to an hour. The drier the better.
- When tofu is sufficiently drained, start warming up the oil. If using a pan, make sure the oil is deep enough to envelop the tofu when placed in the oil.
- Have 3 nicely sized containers, like Tupperware containers or casserole dishes. In one container mix the flour, cornstarch, pepper and salt.
- In the second, beat up the Egg Beaters for an egg wash.
- In the third container, mix the bread crumbs and crushed red pepper.
- Dice the tofu into nice bite-size chunks.
- Coat the tofu in the flour mixture. Sometimes it is nice to have a Tupperware container with a top so you can just shake up the tofu in the mixture.
- Then coat the tofu with the egg, to help hold everything together.
- Finally, coat them with the breadcrumbs and they should be ready for frying.
- If the oil pops when you splash a drop of water in it, it is ready. Fry tofu to a nice golden brown.
- Place on a dish with paper towels to drain excess oil.

notes:

Spinach Salad

Ingredients:
- 1–2 bunches of spinach. Can buy fresh spinach already cleaned and in bags at some groceries.
- 2 fresh vine tomatoes
- 10 fresh mushrooms, thinly sliced
- Feta cheese to taste

Method:
- Clean and assemble the above ingredients.
- Add the tofu around the edge of the salad and serve the Thai sauce on the side. This flavor combination is incredible.

This is the best flavor combination I've found with the tofu and Thai sauce.

Bananas Foster

Ingredients:
- vanilla ice cream
- 5 or 6 ripe bananas
- 1 cup brown sugar
- 1 tablespoon butter, or margarine
- 1/2 cup Bourbon, or brandy

Method:
- Heat brown sugar and butter to a liquid consistency.
- Cut up bananas and add to hot mixture. Sauté briefly.
- Add the Bourbon or brandy, stir around a bit. Then, with a match, light the mixture. The alcohol will burn with a nice blue flame.
- Pour mixture over vanilla ice cream and eat while still warm. Be ready for the hot bananas to melt the ice cream. I don't think you will mind.

No trumpets sound when the important decisions in your life are made. Destiny is made known silently.

Agnes DeMille

Garland McNully

Little Rock, AR

I don't wait for moods.
You accomplish nothing if you
do that. Your mind must know it
has got to get down to earth.

Pearl S. Buck

Garland McNully

Newly married, 1947

My beautiful children–Hollis, James, Annabelle, 1960

I was born in Sevier County, Arkansas, in the southwestern corner of the state. There were six of us children of a loving mother and dad. I had two brothers and three sisters, with me being next to the youngest. My fondest childhood memories are of all of us at home around the dinner table.

I graduated from high school during World War II. A friend and I were recruited and tested for jobs with the United States Treasury Department. We both got jobs, traveling by train for two days to get to Washington, D.C., where we were going to work. Since soldiers had priority on available train seats, my girlfriend and I stood or sat on our luggage during the trip, and at times even sat on the floor. Airline travel wasn't available. My friend and I lived in northwest Washington D.C. in a large boarding house with boys on one side of the dining room and gals on the other side.

I moved from Washington, D.C. to Orange, Texas, at the end of 1945. My mother was ailing and asked that I come home. Dad was working in one of the wartime shipyards there. I went to work for the U.S. Employment Service. Here I met and married a tall, handsome Texan. We had three beautiful children, a daughter Annabelle, and two sons, my oldest child Hollis and his younger brother James. My husband's work took him to Utah, where we lived for six years. His job was very stressful, and he died of a heart attack while on the job. The children and I moved back to Texas; Hollis was ten, Annabelle was eight, and James just two.

After living in Texas for a year, we were forced by Hurricane Carla to leave the area. Returning to a home filled with water and mud, we decided we didn't like the Gulf Coast area and returned to Arkansas. I built a home and planned to live life there forever.

The small town where we lived offered very little for summer employment or entertainment to occupy the kids' time or energy. So, I built a public swimming pool and concession stand on the acreage I owned back in

Cooking something up in the kitchen with my wonderful husband, Dave, 1998.

Dave as Raggedy Ann and me as Raggedy Andy, changing roles for Halloween, Bel Air, MD, 1979.

Texas. Each summer the kids and I went there to have some fun, while at the same time teaching the kids about responsibility and what it meant to work. At the end of each summer, we closed the pool, heading home in time for the kids to return to school.

After living in Arkansas for five years, I met a super nice bachelor schoolteacher and married him. A few years after we married, Dave left teaching and took a civil service job in public affairs with the U.S. Army. We moved to El Paso, Texas, where he commuted to his job at White Sands Missile Range in New Mexico. We lived in El Paso for six years, and there I learned to love

Making daughter's double wedding ring quilt, 1989.

My dear grandchildren: Lauren, Georgia, Brandon, Kristin – 1992

Mexican food. From El Paso, we moved to Bel Air, Maryland. Our home was near the Aberdeen Proving Grounds where my husband Dave worked. We lived there about two years before getting the opportunity to return to Arkansas. Dave took a job with the U.S. Army Corps of Engineers in Little Rock. We considered

this move to be our final move and built a home on 7.5 acres of land a few miles outside North Little Rock. We've lived here over 20 years and on December 27, 2000, we celebrated our 35th wedding anniversary. Our children are grown, having graduated from high school and college. All are happily married. We have four beautiful and healthy grandchildren, although only one lives nearby.

I've had several hobbies, but the main two are cooking and sewing. At one time I sewed nearly everything my daughter and I wore. I was also interested in quilting. I pieced and quilted each of my children a quilt, as well as worked on a couple my mother had pieced together. I've enjoyed collecting Heisey crystal (orchid pattern), cookbooks, teapots, blue plates, and cowbells. I'm not really an avid collector of any of these anymore.

I look back on my life with satisfaction. I have a wonderful family and many friends from every place I've lived. In 2000, I attended my 57th graduating class reunion.

Garland McNulty

Garland's Menu

- Spinach and Artichokes in Puff Pastry
- Chardonnay Wine
- Chicken Pillows
- Green Beans Almondine
- Candied Yams
- Green Pea Salad
- Rolls and Butter
- Water and Iced Tea
- Blueberry Bavarian Pie

notes:

Dinner with Goddess Garland

My early memories are filled with family gatherings and nutritious home-cooked meals. My first six years of life were during the Depression, and often there was a lack of food staples that we had come to count on, such as flour and sugar.

We were blessed to live in the country and grew most of our own food. We had chickens and eggs, a vegetable garden and a fruit orchard with peaches, apples and pears. Dad also grew corn that became our staple to replace flour. Dad would go to a gristmill to bring home corn meal so we could make cornbread and muffins. Because we were so young, all we understood was that we missed our regular bread and biscuits.

Even though we lived through the Depression, I always felt secure because of the love in my family. There was never a question that we would share everything. Sharing good food with family and friends is still something we do as often as we can.

When I am planning a meal for family and friends, I always think first about the people. I like to gather friends who would be comfortable being together, who could enjoy each other while I did last-minute things. It gives me joy to listen to people visiting. I have always loved the simple pleasures in life. Still do.

Spinach and Artichokes in Puff Pastry

Ingredients:
- (1) 10 ounce package frozen chopped spinach, thawed
- (1) 14 ounce can artichoke hearts, drained and chopped
- 1/2 cup mayonnaise
- 1/2 cup Parmesan cheese, grated
- 1 teaspoon onion powder
- 1 teaspoon garlic powder
- 1/2 teaspoon pepper
- (1) 17.3 ounce package frozen puff pastry

Method:
- Thaw puff pastry at room temperature for 30 minutes.
- Drain spinach well, pressing between layers of paper towels.
- Stir together spinach, artichoke hearts and next 5 ingredients.
- Unfold pastry and place on lightly floured surface or heavy-duty plastic wrap.
- Spread one-half of spinach mixture evenly over pastry sheet, leaving a 1/2 inch border.
- Roll up pastry, jellyroll fashion, pressing to seal seam. Wrap in heavy-duty plastic wrap.
- Repeat procedure with remaining pastry and spinach mixture.
- Freeze 30 minutes; cut into 1/2 inch thick slices. (Rolls may be frozen unsliced for up to 3 months. Take from freezer and let set in refrigerator for a few hours for ease in slicing.)
- Bake at 400° for 20 minutes or until golden brown.
- Yield: 4 dozen.

Chicken Pillows

Ingredients:
- 6 boneless chicken breast halves
- 6 slices Proscuitto, thinly sliced
- 6 slices Swiss cheese, thinly sliced
- 6 tablespoons butter or margarine, melted
- 6 tablespoons Italian breadcrumbs
- 6 tablespoons medium dry sherry
- 2 tablespoons chopped parsley, fresh or dried
- salt and pepper to taste

Method:
- Pre-heat oven to 350°.
- Lightly grease shallow baking dish.
- Pound chicken breast halves until thin and tender.
- On each breast half lay one slice cheese, one slice Proscuitto, and one tablespoon breadcrumbs.
- Roll up, starting at broader end, and secure with toothpicks.
- Roll in Italian breadcrumbs and place in baking dish.
- Combine sherry and butter.
- Pour over chicken.
- Salt and pepper to taste.
- Sprinkle with parsley.
- Bake approximately 45 minutes (until chicken is done).

notes:

Green Beans Almondine

Ingredients:
- 1 pound frozen cut green beans
- 1/4 teaspoon salt, to taste
- 1/2 cup slivered almonds

Method:
- Cook beans in microwaveable dish according to directions on the bag. (I find it takes green beans longer to cook than is called for on most bags.)
- When beans are about half cooked, add salt and almonds.

Candied Sweet Potatoes

Ingredients:
- 6 medium sweet potatoes
- 1/3 cup brown sugar, packed
- 1/4 cup crushed pineapple, drained
- 1 teaspoon vanilla
- 4 tablespoons margarine
- 3 tablespoons rum or orange juice

Method:
- Pre-heat oven to 350°.
- Boil sweet potatoes until almost done. Drain well and let cool.
- Peel and cut potatoes into 1/2 inch slices.
- Arrange slices, slightly overlapping, in a buttered shallow baking dish.
- Spread pineapple on top of sweet potatoes.
- Dot with butter, then sprinkle evenly with brown sugar.
- Mix vanilla with rum or orange juice and drizzle over brown sugar.
- Bake uncovered for 30 minutes or until bubbly and glazed.

Green Pea Salad

Ingredients:
- 1 pound frozen peas, thawed
- 1 small can chopped smoked almonds
- 2 or 3 green onions, diced (optional)
- 1 (8) ounce can sliced water chestnuts, chopped
- 1 cup mayonnaise

Method:
- Mix all ingredients together.
- Put in bowl lined with lettuce leaves.
- Top with small amount of grated cheddar cheese.

notes:

Blueberry Bavarian Pie

This recipe was originally for two pies, but they were skimpy and there wasn't enough blueberry topping for two. I make one larger, fuller pie with enough blueberry topping to cover well, then use the extra filling and topping for dessert at another meal.

Ingredients:
- 1 pie crust, baked and cooled
- 1 pkg. Dream Whip
- 1 8 ounce pkg. cream cheese
- 2 bananas
- 1 large can blueberry pie filling
- 1 cup sugar
- Cool Whip or whipped cream for decoration (optional)

Method:
- Mix Dream Whip according to directions on package. Set aside.
- Mix together cream cheese (at room temperature) and sugar.
- Add to Dream Whip mixture.
- Slice bananas into pie crust.
- Pour about three-fourths of cream cheese/ Dream Whip mixture over bananas in crust and top with blueberry pie filling.
- Decorate with Cool Whip or whipped cream around outer edge of pie, if desired.
- Keep pie refrigerated.

One can never consent to creep

when one feels an impulse to soar.

Helen Keller

Jean Perrine

Walterboro, SC

*Life is what you make it,
always has been, always will be.*

Grandma Moses

Jean Perrine

Me and Tiddley - Circa 1957

Celebrating at a goddess gathering, 1994.

I am an adventuress at heart. I enjoy doing physical things because it gives me a tangible sense of accomplishment. From simple things like gardening to life-changing experiences like spending ten years in Saudi Arabia, I always look for the adventure.

When I was growing up in northern California, there were very few children, and I always sort of felt left out. I yearned for friends and found my first one in a horse. I was fascinated with horses. In my eyes there was no such thing as a less than excellent one. I loved them all, and wanted to keep every one I saw.

69

So I began riding at a young age and this gave me a sense of freedom. I was independent and mobile way before I was old enough to drive a car. Just getting out of the house and meeting up with friends for 'Cowboys and Indians' was thrilling to me. It may seem funny, but I still do the same thing today.

I met and married Spencer, my best friend since grade school. He had the same interest in horses as I did, living in the same 'cowboy' country in the interior of northern California. Our life together has been filled with adventures because of where

My daughters and me -– left to right: Monta, me, Sonia – 1996

he has flown, all over the world. The most interesting location we lived was in Saudi Arabia. My husband, two daughters and I were in a compound in the desert near the Red Sea. I learned an enormous amount about human nature and found that with few exceptions, there is no right or wrong, simply different ways of doing things. People are the same everywhere. They have the same worries, cares and hopes as we do. Most important, I learned that a smile is a smile in any language.

As my daughters have grown and moved on to create their own lives, I have reflected on the joy of being their mom. Each has a life that suits her perfectly. The birth of my daughters turned my life around, from an isolated adolescent to a fulfilled woman. To this day, each time we are able to be together I experience great joy. We always have such a wonderful time together, even if it is only for a few hours.

Most changes strike me as a potential new adventure, and I'm ready to jump into something new. Or out of it. Like the time I jumped out of an airplane. It was in November of 2000. I did a skydive in tandem with a jump master. We jumped from the plane at 10,000 feet and were free falling for 5,000 feet before opening the chute. Once it opened, we gently floated all around the sky, making circles and zigzags before landing. We actually landed standing up. It was totally unreal and exciting. It made me feel even more alive.

Feeling glamorous, 2001

I actually joined the Cavalry recently. During the Civil War the Cavalry was responsible for clearing the way for the foot soldiers and artillery. Today we have elaborate reenactment teams that represent the North and the South, and we literally act out different battles. It's wild. I never learned so much about life in Civil War days until now! And, by the time I finish applying a bit of makeup, I look like another 'trooper'. It's really an honor to be asked to ride in the Cavalry, especially for me, since there were no women in the original Cavalry and authenticity is a major requirement. From horse tack and uniforms to black powder guns, it's all accurate to the period. It's a unique experience and I enjoy the camaraderie and expert horsemanship required.

My husband Spencer and me at a wedding on the Blue Ridge Parkway, 1994

The Press & Standard newspaper clipping for an award as Operations Manager for the Walterboro Airport, 1999

I've been an animal lover forever and I'm always at home in nature. Nature's rhythms deeply soothe me and I experience immediate understanding on non-verbal levels. When I feel out of balance, all I do is walk through the woods with my six dogs and watch them hunt 'monsters'... or swim in ponds and chase each other. Within minutes, I begin to feel better. Just being outside with the trees, plants or whatever 'critter' runs across the path has a lovely calming effect on me. It works every time.

Another simple pleasure I enjoy is to sit on our deck and watch the light show of clouds and colors, as the sun sinks into the horizon. These lovely sunsets are new and different every evening. It's really a free show for anyone who'll take the time to watch the subtle changes that unfold.

Jean Perrine

Jean's Menu

- Chips and Dip
- Fresh Veggies and Dip
- Tossed Green Salad
- Mushroom Chicken Casserole
  over Rice
- White Wine
- Ice Cream Sandwich Layered Cake

notes:

Dinner with Goddess Jean

You can always count on an easy style in my house. I like easy preparation, casual dining, flexible timing and a 'going with the flow' attitude. So my menu is simple, yet tasty. I like to have most things prepared ahead of time so I can visit rather than cook while friends are over for dinner.

I didn't think it was necessary to give you guidance on my appetizers, or the making of a tossed green salad. If I have my main dish handled, I'm pretty flexible about the rest. It depends on the mood I am in.

Mushroom Chicken Casserole

Ingredients:
- 3 pounds boneless, skinless chicken breasts
- 12 ounce package of fresh mushrooms cleaned and sliced into about three pieces each
- 12 ounce pack of shredded cheese. Mozzarella is good, or I also like the Italian blend
- (1) 10 ounce can, cream of celery soup
- (1) 10 ounce can, cream of mushroom
- garlic powder to taste
- black pepper to taste, freshly ground
- 6 tablespoons olive oil

Method:
- Pre-heat oven to 325°.
- Mix the two cans of soup together. Do not add water.
- Cut chicken into fairly small pieces (approximately 3 1/2 inches square) and sprinkle with garlic powder and fresh ground pepper, to your own taste.
- In a large non-stick frying pan, heat 4 tablespoons olive oil. Turning pan to medium-low, cook chicken until each piece is lightly browned. Set aside.
- Add 2 tablespoons olive oil and 1 tablespoon water to the same frying pan and sauté the mushrooms for about 5 minutes.
- Add onions and continue cooking, covered, until onions are just tender.

- Using a 9" X 12" casserole dish, layer all the ingredients. First the chicken, then add mushrooms and onions, cheese, and finally a layer of the soup mixture. Keep going until all ingredients have been used. Finish with a topping of the soup mixture.

- Bake for 35 to 40 minutes to blend all the ingredients together. Serve with, or over, the rice you have selected.

Ice Cream Sandwich Layered Cake

Ingredients:
- 8 to 10 ice cream sandwiches
- 1 large container of Cool Whip
- 4 to 6 Heath candy bars, or Butterfinger candy bars

Method:
- Layer a dish with ice cream sandwiches.
- Cover this layer with Cool Whip.
- Do another layer of ice cream sandwiches.
- Do another layer of Cool Whip.
- Top with crushed candy bars.
- Keep in freezer, covered.
- Slice in squares and serve.

notes:

To keep our faces toward change and behave
like free spirits in the presence of fate
is strength undefeatable.

Helen Keller

Jill Abbyad

New Orleans, LA

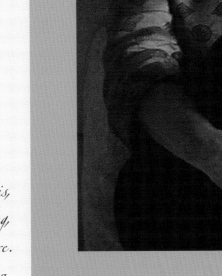

The trouble is,
if you don't risk anything,
you risk even more.

Erica Jong

Jill Abbyad

13 years old, Southern California, 1961

Living in Los Angeles, 1976

I was born in Ohio, where I learned I did not want to live in cold weather. My family—parents and two sisters—relocated to southern California in 1958, setting my spirit free. Body surfing introduced me to fluid physical sensations and going with the flow of life. My teenage years were marred by a series of unfortunate events, including the divorce of my parents. I was raised Christian, and both parents remarried into the Jewish faith within two years. Both the divorce and the remarriages further splintered my family.

I was a dancer and retreated into fantasy realms. Late night radio in Los Angeles opened my mind to cultures beyond what I knew or could see, listening to what is now referred to as 'root music' (indigenous people's music) at a very impressionable age. My father gave me the gift of Jazz, my mother the gift of Opera. When I was a child my mother, Doris, sang live on the radio.

After graduating high school, I relocated to the San Francisco Bay area where I attended college and bought my first car (VW Bug), both fueling my sense of freedom. Supporting myself and putting my younger sister through high school gave me strength, self-assurance, discernment and the knowledge that something was protecting me. Meeting Pamela (the creator of this book) in 1966 began my most influential friendship. When we were together, our layers were revealed to the core, bringing rich substance and clarity of purpose up for review. We explored what 'that something' was that was protecting us. We became soul companions and will forever be.

Another favorite yoga posture, 1998

Honeymoon with my husband, Charles, 1985

galaxy', teaching me how to love, among a wealth of other lessons. One important lesson I learned was to never abandon myself, never lose myself, or forget who I am. Living in Hollywood and working in the music business filled with enthusiasm, glamour, and self-motivation gave me the tools to get both feet on the ground very quickly. I learned that flaunting, bragging and showing-off are traits I'd rather not have in my life. It was time to move on.

I've always engaged life fully. I spent three months traveling with friends, from Portugal to Morocco. I used every form of transportation, learning the ways of the world. Over the next several years, I studied dance, movement of the stars, meditation, metaphysics, massage therapy, philosophy, yoga, literature and Asian

Doing what I love, 1998

Falling deeply in love for the first time (with a dancer) during my mid-20's brought full womanhood to life. I was now seized by a brand new 'guide to the culture. Asian culture was, and is now, ever present in my life. I was one of five Americans who worked for a Japanese trading firm in Los Angeles for six years. There I learned some different thinking skills and problem-solving techniques. One gift I received from working with this Japanese company was to consider outcomes that encompass one's country and business as a whole, rather than focusing on an individual point of view. It helped me get outside myself, expanding my abilities to see the bigger picture in most life situations.

Radical changes were the keynote at this point in my life. While working for a computer company in California, I was sent to Louisiana for one year. I managed to meet some extraordinary southern females who helped my sojourn into uncharted waters. After agreeing to stay two more years, I met a gentleman of consequence in New Orleans. Charles had everything on my wish list and more!

Charles had lived in Beirut, although his family came from Palestine. His parents also came to live in New Orleans, when the war intensified in Beirut in the early 80's. Charles' family is by far the most functional,

My beloved family – Yasmin, Charles, Xander and me, 1998

positive and supportive family I've ever experienced. They have a grip on what is important in life—Love. During the first six months of our relationship, both Charles and I said farewell to a parent. Through the process of a parent dying, we shared the depths of pain and the joys of life with one another, falling deeply in love. We married, bought a house and created 'The Chimes Bed and Breakfast' in New Orleans. Two beloved children were born to us, Yasmin and Xander, now in their early teens. Charles is the Maitre D' at Arnaud's Restaurant in the French Quarter.

After helping the city create a bed and breakfast ordinance, we began a renovation. Due to an architect's error, our 1876 house/business had to be dismantled and rebuilt. This project, and ensuing court case, was yet another example of holding fast to the belief in truth and inner strength. We were proven correct after a six-year court case. From this, I learned the depths of my mate's core being. Charles handled this immense legal challenge with his usual dignity and strength. This kind of beauty comes from deep within one's soul.

My life is full of much love. I learn something every day, expanding my understanding about life. I spend my days managing our bed and breakfast, practicing yoga and enjoying my husband and children. I know I am a child of God, divine with energy flowing through me, helping to create my life as it is today.

You can contact Jill at the Chimes Bed and Breakfast at: www.chimesbandb.com

79

Jill's Menu

- Chips and Dip
- Hommus with Toasted Pita Wedges
- Wine
- Rice with Meat and Yogurt
- Tabbouleh
- Jill's Lemon Soy chicken
- Yogurt Cheese with Pita Wedges
- Coffee
- Seasonal Fruit

notes:

Dinner with Goddess Jill

At the Abbyad dinner table, we always have at least our two children, Charles and myself. We like to talk, share ideas, make plans and use this time to reflect on actions and events.

Charles and I usually each have a glass of wine. I have chosen two everyday wines that would complement my offering – Le Crema Pinot Noir or Silverado Chardonnay.

Hommus

This dish is used many ways in the Arabic tradition. For this meal, I am using it as a dip, eaten with toasted pita bread. Hommus is also served with chicken or meat for dipping, as a main dish. If you have hommus in your refrigerator, you will never be without something delicious to eat.

Ingredients:
- Pre-heat oven to 400°.
- 1 can chickpeas. If you want to use dried chickpeas, soak overnight and then boil for 1 1/2 hours.
- 2 tablespoons Tahini (raw sesame oil purchased at a Middle Eastern store, or your own supermarket). Do not use toasted sesame oil.
- 1/2 cup fresh lemon juice. Add more for your own taste.
- 1 teaspoon salt
- 1 or 2 large cloves of garlic, crushed
- 1 HOT pepper, chopped fine. Can also use cayenne pepper.
- 1/2 cup freshly chopped parsley
- 3 pieces of pita bread, cut into smaller pieces, separated, and toasted in your pre-heated oven.

notes:

notes:

Method:
- Boil chickpeas in water until they are tender, even if you are using canned peas.
- Drain and mash chickpeas while hot in a food mill or electric blender, leaving out a few whole ones for decoration.
- Let cool a bit.
- Blend in the Tahini, lemon juice, garlic, salt and mix well.
- Add a little cold water to give a white color to the Tahini.
- Beat the mixture until the puree is smooth and has a creamy consistency.
- Adjust the seasoning to your taste. Add more lemon juice, salt and pepper, if needed.
- Pour mixture into an oval plate, spread and garnish with chopped parsley and the whole chickpeas you saved earlier.
- Serve the toasted pita bread in a basket near the Hommus.

Nellie's Yogurt

Everyone would love and appreciate my mother-in-law, Nellie, if they knew her. She was raised in Palestine and educated in a Catholic girls' school in Jerusalem. With all she has been through, there is no sign of bitterness. Only kind, loving actions and thoughts emanate from her being; therefore, I take her comments and expressions in that spirit.

When my husband and I bought our house, Nellie helped me settle in. When the yogurt maker was unpacked she asked what it was. After I explained, she chuckled and said, "You Americans are so silly." I replied, "How do you make yogurt?" The following day she returned to help, with rubber gloves and the ingredients for making yogurt. She said, "Today I will teach you how to make yogurt our way."

She boiled the milk (one gallon), turned off the fire, and waited for it to cool. She waited until she could put her finger in the milk and count to ten, without being burned. At that point, when the milk was not too hot or too cold, it was ready to receive the 'starter,' a small container of Nellie's favorite plain yogurt. She slowly added the 'starter' to the milk, smoothing the lumps until all the 'starter' and milk were blended.

Then came the most amazing step. She covered the pan, wrapped it in a wool blanket and put it under the bed. Nellie explained that the wool would hold the warmth around the mixture, while putting it under the bed would keep it out of my way. She claimed that in twenty-four hours we would have a gallon of fabulous yogurt. Indeed, we unwrapped the blanket, uncovered the pan and tasted the most delicious tart creamy substance I'd ever eaten. I was truly impressed. That very day I gave away my yogurt maker, becoming an 'under-the bed' yogurt convert.

Yogurt (Laban in Arabic)

The yogurt recipe I'm offering is a slightly revised version. Although, if your kitchen is small or you don't have a pilot light on your stove, Nellie's method will always work. After completing this yogurt recipe, I will then teach you a process used to make yogurt cheese for spreading on bread.

Ingredients:
- 1 gallon (or quart) of milk; the portions are not critical when making yogurt.
- 3 heaping tablespoons of plain yogurt.
- 1 teaspoon salt

Method:
- Bring the milk to a boil. Remove it from the heat and allow it to cool until you can put your finger in it and count to ten without having to remove your finger, approximately 90° F.
  Thin out the starter with warm milk as you add it. Cover and leave it on the top of a gas stove with a pilot light, or put in another warm place. (Wrapped in a wool blanket under the bed works well, too.)
- Remove in approximately twenty-four hours. Uncover, add salt and stir.
- Fill a large jar with the finished yogurt and refrigerate.

notes:

82

Yogurt Cheese
(Lebneh in Arabic)

If you want something wonderful to do with the leftovers…read on. You can now use some of the yogurt you made for yogurt cheese, similar to cream cheese in consistency. This cheese can be served with fresh tomatoes, olives, goat cheese and pita bread for a complete meal. It is a yummy spread on bread.

Method:
- Use a cheesecloth bag, a muslin bag with a string or a pillowcase. Pour the remaining yogurt in a corner of the bag.
- Tie the bag and hang it over a pan overnight to drip the water out, leaving a thick creamy consistency. Turn the bag inside out and put this cheese in a container and refrigerate.

Rice with Meat and Yogurt

If you have no interest in making your own yogurt, buy your favorite brand for this dish. I use nonfat yogurt with live acidophilus from the health food store. It also contains live bulgaricus, thermophilus and bifidum. Yogurt used with rice dishes is the more liquid yogurt, not the cheese. This dish can be refrigerated, and then reheated.

Ingredients:
- 1 large yellow onion, diced into 1/2" pieces
- 1 pound lean ground meat
- 2 cups brown Basmati rice (any rice can be substituted and cooked accordingly)
- 1/2 cup blanched almonds, chopped or slivered
- 1 tablespoon olive oil
- 1 teaspoon olive oil
- 1/8 teaspoon butter
- 1 teaspoon salt
- 1 teaspoon ground allspice
- 1 teaspoon onion powder
- 1/2 teaspoon cinnamon
- 1 can beef broth (approximately 2 cups)
- 2 1/2 cups water (or equal parts rice and liquid, if using white rice)

Method:
- Use a large sauté pan with a lid. Add 1 teaspoon olive oil and a small pat of butter (for flavor only) into the sauté pan and heat.
- Add slivered almonds and toss to evenly toast. When brown, remove from pan and put aside.
- Add 1 tablespoon olive oil, heat and add chopped onions. Sauté on medium to high heat until edges are browned.
- Tear ground meat into pieces and sauté with onions after they are browned. Drain fat if necessary.
- Sprinkle allspice, onion powder, cinnamon, salt and pepper into mixture. Stir together.
- Measure beef broth in measuring cup; add enough water to equal 4 1/2 cups of liquid. Pour into pan over meat and onions and bring to a boil.
- Add rice, stir, cover and cook for approximately 40 minutes if using brown rice (follow time instructions on the rice package). Cook on low heat until all water is absorbed and rice grains are popped open.
- Season to taste.
- Put in serving bowl and sprinkle toasted almonds over the top.
- Serve beside a bowl of yogurt.
- Spoon yogurt over rice on serving plates.

Tabbouleh

Parsley is one of the most nourishing dark green leaves on the planet, and this is a tasty way to enjoy it. This recipe calls for lots of parsley and little wheat, unlike some other country's Tabbouleh. This is a beautiful herb to grow in your garden all winter. It thrives in colder weather. I find four plants keep us in salad during the winter months. Charles' custom is to eat salad after dinner to flood the digestive track with roughage.

Ingredients:
- 4 large bunches parsley, washed, large stems removed, and dried (This step can be done a few days ahead. Wrap in cotton towel and placed in a plastic bag in the refrigerator.)
- 1 bunch green onion, diced
- 3/4 cup dry Burghol (crushed wheat #1) I usually find this in a health food or Middle Eastern store (#1 is a fine grind, #2 course and #3 very course.)
- 2 large or 3 small ripe tomatoes, diced
- 1 tablespoon dried mint or 2 tablespoons fresh mint
- 1/2 cup fresh lemon Juice or more to taste (we use enough to make the salad juicy)
- 2/3 cup olive oil
- 1 head Romaine lettuce, washed and bottom trimmed, about 1 1/2 inches
- salt and pepper to taste, (I use coarsely ground.)

Method:
- Soak Burghol (or wheat) in water in a strainer. Remove from water and let stand for fifteen minutes and drain.
- Chop dried parsley finely by hand with a sharp large knife OR put it in the food processor. Place in a large bowl.
- Wash and chop green onions and tomatoes and add them to the parsley.
- Add drained wheat (should be dry but soft and expanded). Toss all together.
- Add mint, lemon juice, olive oil, salt and pepper. Blend well.
- Season to taste. This means if the parsley sticks in your mouth, add olive oil. If it's tasteless, add more lemon, salt and pepper. One must play with taste here because portions are difficult to determine.
- Serve on a platter with Romaine leaves surrounding the edges of the platter. Spoon the Tabbouleh onto the middle of the platter with the Romaine leaves jutting out from underneath.
- Individuals can take the portions they want, spooning onto large Romaine lettuce leaves.

Jill's Soy Lemon Chicken

Although I blended these flavors on my own, I do not remember what dish inspired the idea. However, I'm sure it was something Asian, my favorite food.

If you like chicken, yet do not have the time to prepare food like you were having a spiritual experience, then you will be a fan of this offering. It's quick, easy and delicious, tasting more complex than it really is. Then you will have time for that spiritual experience, which hopefully will be equally as easy and delicious.

Besides the menu I have offered, I often serve this chicken dish with rice, pasta, potatoes or just vegetables. You can also substitute pork chops using the exact same ingredients and procedures. I use two skillets and make a large quantity to use as leftovers, which are almost as good as the first time around.

notes:

Ingredients:
- 1 whole chicken (or equivalent in pieces) cut up.
- 2 tablespoons Tamari or soy sauce I use one with reduced sodium
- 3 tablespoons FRESH lemon juice – (approximately 3 lemons, depending on the season)
- 1 teaspoon crushed and dried, or 2 teaspoons fresh rosemary
- 2 teaspoons olive oil
- 1/2 cup flour
- 1 1/2 cups water

Method:
- Skin, wash and dry chicken pieces. Sprinkle with seasoning salt of your choice. I use Paul Prudhommes' Magic Seasoning Salt.
- Prepare a plate with the flour evenly spread and lightly dust chicken with a coating of flour.
- Heat 2 teaspoons of olive oil in a large skillet. Brown chicken well on medium to high heat, until all sides are very brown, (approximately 15 minutes, depending on the skillet used).
- Pour a mixture of 2 tablespoons of Tamari sauce and 3 tablespoons of fresh lemon juice over chicken. It will steam and bubble up. Add water and loosen chicken from pan bottom, if necessary.
- Toss in the rosemary.
- Cover and let chicken steam on low to medium heat for approximately 35 minutes or until chicken is falling off the bone. You may add more water if pan dries out before chicken is done. If gravy is too thin, remove lid and cook a few minutes uncovered.
- Serve with a sprig of fresh rosemary on each plate or on top of the serving dish. Don't let the ingredient of rosemary stop you from preparing this dish. It's still great without it.

Someone said that life is a party.

You join in after it's started

and leave before it's finished.

Elsa Maxwell

Kathy Becknell

Fayetteville, GA

Too much of a good thing can be wonderful.

Mae West

Kathy Becknell

With my dear husband, Mark, at our daughter Lauren's 1st birthday party, 1999

Sophomore in High School, one of my happiest years, Florida 1982

My biography format is two-fold. The first part lists the dates and details on how my life unfolded. The second part are answers to the questions Pamela asked each of us goddesses, as a way of sharing the highlights of our lives.

I was born in Miami, Florida, and was adopted three months later. I grew up in Fort Myers, Florida. I left home at 19 to attend the University of Florida. I got married at age 20, and had my son, Ryan, at age 21. We moved to Tennessee in 1987, where I attended nursing school at the University of Tennessee in Memphis. I graduated in 1990. My daughter Ashten was born that same year. We moved to New Jersey for a one-year stay, before moving back to Florida. Soon after the move I got a divorce.

In 1992, I was a single mom starting over in Atlanta. I met my husband, Mark, in 1995. We celebrated our wedding day in October of 1997. I had my third child, daughter Lauren, that next December in 1998. I just gave birth to my fourth child, daughter Claire, in March 2002.

Dancing in a nightclub in Rome, Italy, 2001

My courage is challenged:

• By trying to be a wife, mother, housekeeper, cook, gardener, nurse, chauffeur, lover and friend – in other words, being a domestic goddess. I find it difficult to pull off all of these roles with calmness, organization and flair, without being exhausted. I am constantly striving for harmony and balance in my life.

• In my search for the 'perfect' job. I desire to be of service to people, while also using my creative and expressive abilities. I do not want this to take away from my family life. I would like to feel I am using my God-given talents to achieve financial success, while sensing peace and satisfaction.

Some of my most joyful moments:

• My first kiss.

• The day I was accepted into a sorority.

• When I found out I was pregnant, all four times.

• When my husband Mark proposed to me.

• When I graduated college with honors.

• When I found out who my biological family was, and the circumstances for my adoption.

• When each of my children was born.

• When we purchased our home.

• When my kids receive awards for academic, creative or athletic achievements because I have encouraged these characteristics in them.

• When I learned how to scuba dive.

Happy Reunion with my biological grandfather and uncle – left to right: me, Uncle Jimmy and his wife Charlotte, my mom Mary and dad George, Grandpa's wife JoAnne and Grandpa James, Florida 1985

The hobbies and interests that give me most pleasure:
- Any kind of exercise, being outdoors, doing activities such as walking, gardening, hiking, white water rafting.
- I enjoy reading, cooking, decorating and deep sea diving.
- Traveling is my favorite interest, especially to places where the culture is different from ours, such as Europe.
- I enjoy my female friendships immensely.

The spiritual principles that guide and feed my spirit:
- I pray daily that God will place me where I am needed. I pray that God's will for my life be done, and that I will draw peace from doing this. I strive to be closer to and have a personal relationship with God.
- I believe all women are perfect and beautiful creations, even if at times they don't believe it. I strive to not only increase my own self-confidence, but also to increase self-confidence in my children and my dear friends.

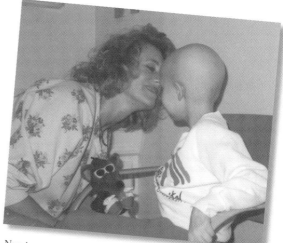

Nursing one of my favorite little oncology patients — Atlanta 1996

- I believe we are whole and complete when our physical, emotional and spiritual aspects are nurtured. Prayer, meditation and public worship help nurture my spiritual side.

This project has impacted me by joyfully allowing part of my creative self to come out. I am happy to collaborate with other wonderful women, with the intention to help all women. I am honored to be part of this project. Cooking is such a fun way to be creative and nurture our bodies. I hope someone will enjoy my contribution to the cookbook. Most importantly, I hope all of the ladies who read our cookbook realize the goddess they are, too. God made every woman beautiful and perfect. Knowing and believing that each of us is beautiful and perfect is essential to becoming the women we are all meant to be.

Kathy Becknell

My wonderful kids—left to right: Ashten, me holding Lauren, and Ryan, 2000

Precious Claire, born March 2002

Kathy's Menu

- Bruschetta
- Wine
- Ice Tea
- 'Beautiful' Salad
- Italian Bread with Dipping Sauce
- Chicken Parmesan
- Linguine with Amy's Sauce
- Almond Biscotti with Vanilla Ice Cream
- Coffee

notes:

Dinner with Goddess Kathy

I am relatively new to cooking with flair, with about five years' experience now. My advice for new cooks is practice, practice and practice. I am thrilled when I can serve a tasty and beautiful dish. First and foremost, food is a blessing from God. Second, preparing food for family and friends is an act of love. As a wife and mother of four, this is one of the most loving things I do for my family. A vivid childhood memory is the aroma of my Mother's spaghetti sauce cooking, and hardly being able to wait until dinnertime. Her sauce was heavenly to me.

Because of my love for everything Italian, I chose an Italian dinner. I believe they have perfected the art of cooking. They savor each course, making meals relaxed and loving. Eating in Italy is a social event, a time for people to bond. They eat very slowly and have high standards for fresh ingredients. While traveling in Italy recently, I was told that fresh ingredients are the magic in making extremely good food. This dinner is for a party of eight. I have gotten rave reviews.

I set the mood for my dinner parties with a lot of candles everywhere. Soft music is nice playing in the background. I like to use my 'good' silver and china because otherwise it sits around and collects dust all year. It is also a way of saying to guests, "you are worth this extra effort." Blessing the food and your guests is a beautiful ritual to God.

Bruschetta

After offering your guests drinks, bring out the bruschetta and let them help themselves. The bruschetta is best when made several days in advance, including the tomato topping. Toast your bread the day of your party so the good smells greet your guests.

Ingredients:
- 4 cloves of garlic, sliced.
- 1 cup olive oil
- 1 loaf of Italian or French bread, sliced thin

Method:
- Place garlic in olive oil.
- Set aside for 1–2 days so the flavors are well mixed.
- Day of party, brush both sides of your French bread with olive oil.
- Broil your bread until toasted.

Tomato Topping Ingredients:
- 6 plum tomatoes, chopped
- 1/4 teaspoon salt
- 1/8 teaspoon pepper
- 1/4 teaspoon fresh basil
- 4 tablespoons olive oil
- 1–2 tablespoons chopped onion

Method:
- Chop tomatoes and set aside.
- Mix all other ingredients and pour over tomatoes.
- Make this ahead of time so the flavors set up and it makes a lot of juice.
- Spoon tomatoes on bread and serve immediately.
- For extra taste, slice fresh Parmesan cheese and place under the tomatoes.
  Or sprinkle fresh shredded Parmesan cheese on top of the tomatoes.

"Beautiful Salad" and Bread

I had an Italian friend named Herb, and whenever he saw a colorful salad he would say, "What a beautiful salad." When I serve the salad and bread, I like to have everyone seated. Italians eat bread freshly baked daily. They slice it, then serve it in a cloth-lined basket. When the salad and bread are served, I would pop the pre-assembled main course into the oven. At this same time, the pasta can go into the water for boiling.

Bread Dipping Sauce

Ingredients:
- 1 cup extra virgin olive oil
- 1/2 teaspoon oregano
- 1/2 teaspoon basil
- pinch of salt
- fresh ground pepper to taste
- 1 cup fresh grated Parmesan

Method:
- Combine all ingredients, except the grated Parmesan.
- Put combined ingredients into shallow bowl for dipping.
- Put Parmesan in a separate bowl for serving on top of the dipped bread.
- Cut up your Italian or French bread into large bite-size pieces that can be easily dipped into the bowls you have placed on the table.

"Beautiful Salad"

Ingredients:
- field greens salad mix
- 4 plum tomatoes
- 1 cup of cabbage
- 1 yellow pepper
- 1/2 red onion, sliced thin
- 2 carrots, sliced thin
- 1 cup croutons
- any other veggie on hand

Method:
- All vegetable preparation can be done earlier in the day.
- Mix all salad ingredients together.
- Salads can be pre-made and served individually, or mixed together in one large bowl, family style.
- Add dressing, toss and serve.

Salad Dressing

Ingredients:
- 1/3 part white balsamic vinegar
- 2/3 parts extra virgin olive oil
- salt and pepper to taste

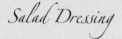

notes:

Amy's Sauce

Jar sauce can be substituted for the homemade recipe. Our friends from Italy came to visit and chose Prego, so I would go with that. I have made this dish both ways, and the homemade sauce is superior. You will have a lot of sauce left over to freeze and use later.

Ingredients:
- 2 medium sized cans or 1 large can tomato sauce
- 3 large cans of whole tomatoes—2 cans hand crushed, 1 can diced
- 2 1/2 cans tomato paste
- 1 1/2 white onions
- 1 teaspoon salt
- 1 tablespoon sugar
- 1/2 teaspoon pepper
- 3 bay leaves, whole
- 1 to 2 crushed bay leaves (crush in your hand)
- 4 cloves garlic (bruise before adding). To bruise, tap with a mallet or end of a knife and put a little dent in the garlic. This allows for more flavor, which is so Italian. Add more garlic if you want
- 1 tablespoon crushed basil leaves (crush by hand)
- 1 teaspoon garlic salt to taste
- 2 tablespoons fresh oregano, chopped

Method:
- Mix all ingredients together and simmer 4 to 8 hours.
- Remove whole bay leaves and garlic before serving.

Chicken Parmesan

If a vegetarian is coming to dinner, eggplant can be a substitute for chicken.

Ingredients:
- 1/2 cup all-purpose flour
- 1/2 cup grated Parmesan cheese
- 1/2 teaspoon black pepper
- 8 (4) ounce skinned, boned chicken breasts
- 2 Large egg whites, lightly beaten
- 2 tablespoons extra virgin olive oil
- cooking spray
- 2 cups (8 ounces) shredded, part-skim mozzarella cheese
- 6 cups hot cooked linguine (about 12 ounces uncooked pasta)

Method:
- Pre-heat oven to 350°.
- Combine flour, Parmesan and black pepper in a shallow dish.
- Place each breast between 2 sheets of heavy-duty plastic wrap; flatten to 1/4 inch thickness using a meat mallet or rolling pin.
- Dip each breast in egg white, dredge in flour mixture.
- Heat olive oil in a large nonstick skillet over medium-high heat.
- Add chicken to skillet; cook 5 minutes on each side or until golden.
- Arrange in baking dish coated with cooking spray.
- Pour tomato sauce over the chicken.
- Sprinkle with mozzarella.
- Bake for 15 minutes.
- Serve over linguine. As soon as the pasta cooks, drain and spoon onto plates. Place chicken on top and garnish with fresh Italian parsley. Serve immediately.

Almond Biscotti

This dessert can be made 1–2 days in advance. Another way to cut back on time is to buy pre-made biscotti at an Italian market. I serve a scoop of vanilla ice cream in a serving dish, adding a biscotti biscuit to the side. I usually have chocolate sauce on the table for anyone who would like it. Extra biscuits can be presented on a pretty platter to be passed for seconds.

Ingredients:
- 2 cups all-purpose flour
- 1 1/2 teaspoons baking powder
- pinch of salt
- 1/3 cup butter (2.7 ounces)
- 1 cup sugar
- zest of 1 lemon, minced
- 3/4 teaspoon almond extract
- 2 large eggs
- 1 cup almonds, chopped

Method:
- Pre-heat oven to 350°.
- Line a baking sheet with parchment paper.
- In a bowl, combine the flour, baking powder, salt and sugar.
- Beat the eggs, one at a time, adding the almond extract.
- Add the dry mixture to the egg mixture and mix well.
- Fold in almonds and mix well.
- Form a log with the dough in the center of a baking sheet pan.
- Bake for 25 minutes.
- Remove from oven and allow to cool for several minutes.
- Turn biscuits over and bake an additional 10 minutes.
- They should be very firm and crunchy. They may need more baking time.
- Cool before serving.

Forgiveness is the key to

action and freedom.

Hannah Arendt

Lea Beyrouthy

Sandy Springs, GA

*Joy is a net of love by
which you can catch souls.*

Mother Teresa

Lea Beyrouthy

Spring in Atlanta with my sister
Grace — Atlanta, 1994

At home in Los Angeles, 1983

I was born in Beirut, Lebanon and lived a good part of my life there. I have been married for more than 46 years, and have three grown daughters who are my pride and joy.

At 22, I married into a family that owned a restaurant serving family-style lunches to lawyers, doctors and other professionals. This restaurant was a historic landmark in the business district of Beirut. It had been in the family since the early part of the century, started by my father-in-law, who was a chef. I loved watching people gather, most customers being regulars and knowing each other. The food was good, healthy, and the generous portions served quickly. Unfortunately, it did not survive the war and was totally destroyed.

Lebanon Beach Resort, 1999

I then started working with my brothers, who were in the jewelry business. I developed a real passion for it. Soon life became unbearable with all the violence around us, and we decided to immigrate to the United States. It took courage to leave everything behind and start over in a new country. Our faith in God gave us the strength to carry on.

We opened a jewelry store in Los Angeles. A few years later we moved to Atlanta and again opened a jewelry store. I enjoy this business, creating my own designs and seeing gemstones turned into works of art. For me, it feels more like a hobby than work.

I also enjoy sewing. Here again I can turn my ideas into reality. I'm glad my daughters ask for my help with the many projects in their homes. My other hobby is cooking. I come from a family of good cooks. Most of our Middle Eastern recipes are passed down from generation to generation. I hope to be able to pass on our recipes to the newest generation in our family.

I'm glad I could participate in this fun project. I enjoy acquainting people with foods that are a part of our culture. And I'm excited to try the menus of the other women in this book.

Atlanta, 2001

With my sister Noha at my niece's wedding, 1998

Lea's
Menu

- Hommus
- Red Snapper with
    Garlic Cilantro Sauce
- Saffron Pilaf Rice
- Baklava

notes:

Dinner with
Goddess
Lea

The memories of my family and the sharing of meals are rich with meaning. The family was our most important bond, so we ate every meal together. I was raised at a time when women stayed in the home, taking care of the meal planning and preparation, the children, the gardens and all other activities involved in sustaining family life.

As part of our Lebanese lifestyle, entertaining was done almost on a daily basis. We would gather among friends and each hostess would try to outdo herself, presenting her guests with the finest gourmet meals. My memories of food, and sharing with family and friends, are love filled. Please enjoy my recipes, knowing they are filled with happiness.

Hommus

Hommus (garbanzo bean dip) can be served as an appetizer with crackers, pita bread chips, or as a side dish next to grilled kebabs (grilled meat or chicken on the skewer).

If hommus is too hard or dry, add more lemon juice or 3 tablespoons water. If hommus is too liquid, put in refrigerator for 2 hours before serving.

Ingredients:
- 2 cups dry garbanzo beans
- 1 teaspoon baking soda
- 1 tablespoon salt
- 2 garlic cloves
- 3/4 cup lemon juice
- 1/4 cup Tahini (ground sesame, available at Middle Eastern specialty food stores)
- cayenne pepper
- olive oil to taste

Method:
- Soak the beans overnight in water with the baking soda.
- Drain beans, cover with water and bring to boil. Pot should be one third full, so as not to overflow.
- Skim foam and reduce heat. Let cook for 1 1/2 hours or until very tender (should be tender enough to smash with a fork).
- Drain and purée garbanzo beans in food processor while still very warm, until smooth and creamy and there are no more lumps.
- Pound garlic until soft, add salt, lemon juice and Tahini. Pour mixture over beans and purée.
- Transfer to a bowl and decorate with cayenne pepper and olive oil.

notes:

Fish Filets with
Garlic Cilantro Sauce

I selected grouper for my recipe because it is a very popular Mediterranean fish. Red snapper would also be a good choice for this recipe.

Cilantro Sauce

Ingredients:
- 1 bunch of cilantro
- 1/2 cup olive oil
- 6 cloves of garlic
- 1 teaspoon salt
- black pepper to taste
- juice of 1 lemon

Method:
- Wash cilantro thoroughly in cold water, as many times as needed to be free of sand. Let drain and dry in salad spinner.
- Mince and pound garlic until soft.
- In food processor, blend cilantro, garlic, salt, pepper, lemon juice and olive oil. You should obtain a smooth, bright green sauce that has the consistency of a salad dressing.

notes:

notes:

Fish

Ingredients:
- 6 boneless, skinless fish fillets
- lemon
- 1 tablespoon salt
- 1 teaspoon pepper
- 6 bay leaves
- 1/2 cup olive oil
- 6 cilantro sprigs
- 1 small yellow onion

Method:
- Pre-heat oven to 400°.
- Rinse fish filets in cold water and let drain. Sprinkle with salt and pepper.
- Peel and cut onion into slices.
- Cut 6 pieces of foil paper (large enough to contain fish filet and close tight).
- In center of each foil paper, lay fish, cover with some olive oil, lemon slice, 1 bay leaf and 1 cilantro sprig.
- Bake for 15–20 minutes, according to fish thickness.
- Arrange fish filets on a platter, cover partially with cilantro sauce.
- Sauce can also be served on the side.
- Decorate with lemon slices.

Saffron Pilaf Rice

This dish was chosen as a side for the fish because of the contrast in colors…the yellow is very appealing next to the white of the fish and bright green of the sauce.

Ingredients:
- 2 tablespoon butter
- 1 cup long grain rice
- 2 cups boiling water
- salt to taste
- 1 level teaspoon powdered saffron
- parsley flakes

Method:
- In a saucepan, bring water to boil.
  Add butter, saffron, salt and rice.
- After it comes to a full boil, reduce heat and simmer covered for about 20 minutes, or until all the water has been absorbed and the rice is tender.
- Transfer the pilaf to a serving plate and dust lightly with parsley flakes.
- Makes 4–6 servings.

Baklava

Sugar Syrup Ingredients:
- 2 cups of granulated sugar
- 1 cup water
- 1 teaspoon lemon juice
- 1/4 cup orange blossom water (sold at Middle Eastern specialty food stores)

Method:
- Stir sugar with water until almost melted and bring to a gentle boil on medium high heat; about 5 minutes.
- Add lemon juice and orange blossom water. Simmer until thick, about 10 minutes. Syrup should have the consistency of maple syrup.

Baklava Ingredients:
- 12"x17" baking tray with rim
- 2 sticks (8 ounces) unsalted butter
- 1 pkg. Fil-O-Dough (16 ounces)
  If frozen, defrost Fil-O-Dough shortly before using.
- 4 cups of ground walnuts mixed with 1 cup of finely granulated sugar
- 1/2 cup of finely chopped unsalted pistachios
- 2 cups of sugar syrup

Method:
- Preheat oven to 325°.
- In the microwave, melt the 2 sticks of butter. Keep warm.
- Butter pan with a pastry brush.
- Take 1 Fil-O-Dough sheet (with extreme care not to tear it) and lay it in the pan, (If sheets are not the same size as the tray, trim them to size with sharp knife.) Keep a dish towel nearby to cover the 'waiting to be used' Fil-O-Dough to keep it from drying out and becoming brittle.
- Brush Fil-O-Dough sheet with butter.
- Repeat the procedure until 1/3 of the Fil-O-Dough package has been used.
- Spread walnut mixture evenly over the dough sheet.
  Sprinkle with some melted butter.
- Lay 1 dough sheet over the walnut mixture and brush with butter.
- Repeat the procedure till you have used all the Fil-O-Dough sheets.
- Brush the top with melted butter.
- With a very sharp knife, cut the uncooked baklava into lozenges, making sure to go all the way through.
- Bake for 30 minutes, then broil 5 minutes at 450° till golden brown.
- Let cool for 5 minutes and sprinkle with sugar syrup
- Let cool completely before taking out of the pan.
- Decorate with chopped pistachios.
- Store baklava pieces in a tin container and close lid tightly. Do not store in refrigerator. Baklava will keep fresh and crispy up to three weeks.

It is more important what's in a woman's face than what's on it.

Claudette Colbert

Lee Gouss

Milburn, NJ

*We are always
the same age inside.*

Gertrude Stein

Lee Gouss

Dancing School Recital,
Circa 1932

High School Twirler, 1943

My name is Lee Gouss and I am a famous ballerina. Or is it a world-renowned movie star? If you asked me when I was a girl what I would be in my life, it is one of these two. As a child, I was given ballet and tap dancing lessons. I also had piano lessons, which went by the wayside. I always liked to be involved in extra activities. I was a 'twirler' for the band in high school. I learned how to twirl when I was a youngster at camp. Being a twirler meant that I was at all the football games and practiced with the band. It was such fun.

I went to Trenton State College in New Jersey and graduated with a degree in Business Education. I also received seven credits towards my Masters Degree at Rutgers University in New Jersey, where I was given a grant for a summer workshop in human relations. Both colleges prepared me for my future life and served me well in numerous ways.

Bernie and me at our college prom, 1948

Me with the children – left to right: Richard, Darlene (Deva), Donna 1958

After World War II, I met the love of my life on a 'blind date.' Blind dates were popular then. After ten dates, we became engaged. We met in November 1947 and were married in September 1948. It was a whirlwind courtship, yet we always knew it was right for us. After graduation, I married Bernie 54 years ago. We were lucky as we have been true soul mates. I then took my place in the real world, living a more traditional lifestyle as a wife, mother, and grandmother.

Our marriage produced three wonderful and unique children—Richie, Donna and Deva. We have two super sons-in-law—Michael and Tony. We also have three loving and affectionate grandchildren—Joshua, Shaun and Nicole—whom we love and enjoy immensely. We have only one regret, all our children and their families live in Atlanta, while we still live in New Jersey. We solved that problem by giving good business to Delta and Continental, and our children doing the same. We are all family-minded. Our greatest joys have been sharing many holidays and special happenings with the family.

Bernie and I still love to get dressed up and go on a romantic dinner date, at least every other month. Often we go into New York City, since theater is a big draw for us. New York offers so much and is very exciting. An ideal day would be to go early to the Metropolitan Museum, then walk in Central Park or window shop on Madison Avenue. We like to dine in one of the many great New York restaurants, before driving home to New Jersey.

My husband and I love to travel. We have traveled much in the United States and Europe. The culture and art of the southwest draws us, so we spend much time in New Mexico and Arizona. We are fascinated with Italy, France, Switzerland and Greece, because they have such history. I have never visited anywhere that I did not say to myself, "I must come back." We have collected art from our many travels, which is displayed in our home. I enjoy playing golf and being outdoors, as well as reading.

A favorite family photo – 1998
Top row, left to right: Michael, Josh, Richie, Shaun, Tony
Bottom row, left to right: Donna, Bernie, me, Nicole, Deva

My love of dancing continues. Each spring I purchase a series of tickets to see the American Ballet Company perform at Lincoln Center in New York City. I am always transported into another world by the magnificent dancing and beautiful music. I still daydream that I am the prima ballerina. I also go into Manhattan and take classes, going to museums and art galleries with a teacher/lecturer. These classes are educational and fascinating, greatly enhancing my appreciation for all types of art.

In addition to family, we have many wonderful and interesting friends. People fascinate me. I am blessed in my life with many special people. It is important to be with them, sharing joys, opinions, problems, world and current events, and having discussions on numerous subjects. They are here for me, and I for them.

Writing my recipes and dinner plan, thinking about my life and sharing it briefly, has made me feel attached to the other goddesses. Although I don't know them, the connection is there. My contact for this project with Goddess Pamela has led to more bonding with her. She always lifts me to a higher plane of achievement and development.

I have tendencies to be spiritually inclined, although my life's journey has taken me into a more earthly and grounded passage. I feel I am where I was meant to be, doing what I was meant to do. I hope you will enjoy sharing my dinner with your family and friends, as much as I do with mine.

Lee Gouse

A favorite couple shot of Bernie and me, 1998

Lee's Menu

- Gourmet Cheeses with Crackers
- Eggplant Appetizer on Pita
- Wine
- Shrimp New Orleans Style
- Linguine with Artichoke Sauce
- Tossed Green Salad w/ Vinaigrette
- Warm French bread
- Chocolate Mousse Pie
- Fresh Fruit
- Coffee or Tea

notes:

Dinner *with* Goddess Lee

I chose to serve my menu as a formal dinner, although it can be served casually also. From time to time I like to have an elegant dinner, using my best china and glassware. I would serve appetizers with drinks in our den, which is cozier for six people.

The table would be set with a beautiful tablecloth, napkins in silver napkin rings, and a fresh flower arrangement with candles on either side. Dinner would be in the dining room, with lights dimmed. Soft classical music would be playing in the background. One CD I especially like is called Weekend Classics—Music for Relaxation.

Bernie would serve both red and white wines, according to each guest's preference. A white wine we like is Pinot Grigio, San Margarita. Red wines we enjoy are Rubesco Lungarotti or Brunello di Montalcino.

Appetizers

I'd begin my meal with cheese and crackers, served decoratively on a platter. Two of my favorite cheeses are Gruyére Reserve and French Camembert. If you want another choice besides crackers, seasoned flat bread is nice. I also like to serve an eggplant appetizer with seasoned pita bread wedges.

Pita Bread

Ingredients:
- 1 to 2 pita rounds
- l/4 cup olive oil
- dash of garlic powder
- l/4 cup of Parmesan cheese

Method:
- Pre-heat oven to 350°.
- Slice the pita bread to open up in half.
- Next cut into bite-size triangles.
- Brush inside with olive oil, sprinkle with garlic powder, and then sprinkle with Parmesan cheese.
- Bake on cookie sheet for 8 or 9 minutes, until crispy and lightly browned.

Eggplant Appetizer

Ingredients:
- 1 large eggplant
- 1 medium onion
- 2 cloves garlic
- 1 green pepper
- 1 red pepper
- 3/4 cups mushrooms
- 1/3 cups olive oil
- 1/4 cup water
- 1/2 teaspoon salt
- 1 small can tomato paste
- 2 tablespoons wine vinegar
- 1/2 teaspoon pepper
- 1/2 teaspoon sugar
- 1/2 cup stuffed olives

Method:
- Take skin off the eggplant, and then cut into bite-size pieces.
- Cut the rest of the vegetables into bite-size pieces also.
- Sauté all the vegetables for about 10 minutes. No oil is needed since veggies give off liquid.
- Blend the second set of ingredients to make a purée.
- Pour the blended mixture over the vegetables in your sauté pan.
- Add the stuffed olives and simmer covered for 30–45 minutes.
- Refrigerate overnight.
  Serve at room temperature.

Vinaigrette Dressing

This dressing is very good, and easy to double. I like to use a glass jar to blend all the ingredients, and then shake well until texture is creamy.

Ingredients:
- 2/3 cup extra virgin olive oil
- 1/3 cup Balsamic vinegar
- 1 clove garlic
- 1 teaspoon Dijon mustard
- 1/8 teaspoon pepper, freshly ground
- 1/4 teaspoon sugar

Method:
- Mince the garlic. I put garlic in a mini Cuisinart type mixer.
- Add oil, vinegar, mustard and pepper, blend until creamy texture.
- Add sugar, blending for a second or two (sugar brings out a good taste).

113

Shrimp New Orleans Style

Ingredients:
- 4 tablespoons unsalted butter
- 1 teaspoon minced garlic
- 1 1/2 pounds large fresh shrimp, peeled
- 2 tablespoons Worcestershire sauce
- 1/2 teaspoon, or more, fresh black pepper
- salt to taste (I don't use it)
- 2 tablespoons lemon juice

Method:
- Put butter in skillet and turn heat to high. When it melts, add garlic, shrimp and Worcestershire sauce.
- Cook, stirring occasionally until sauce is thick and shrimp are uniformly pink, about 5 minutes.
  If sauce threatens to dry out, add 1–2 tablespoons of water.
- When shrimp are done, add pepper (and salt if used) and lemon juice.
- Set aside.

notes:

notes:

Artichoke Sauce

I got this sauce recipe from Grace, my Italian beautician.

Ingredients:
- 1 onion, sliced
- 2 cloves garlic, minced
- 1/2 pound Shitake mushrooms, sliced
- 1 tablespoon capers
- fresh pepper to taste
- 1 tablespoon Scotch
- 1 can artichokes, cut in 1/2 or 1/4, depending on size.
- 2 cans Progresso white clam sauce
- 1/2 cup fresh basil, cut into thin strips; or 1/4 cup dried basil
- 3 tablespoons olive oil

Method:
- Warm olive oil in a sauté pan.
- Sauté onions until golden and soft.
- Add Scotch and Shitake mushrooms; sauté until soft.
- Add capers, pepper, basil, garlic, and sauté a few more minutes, until assimilated.
- Add 2 cans white clam sauce and simmer all together for 15-20 minutes.
- Add artichokes and heat another 5 minutes.
- Then serve over linguine.

Linguine

Ingredients:
- 1 pound fresh linguine, bought in a market that sells homemade pastas.

Method:
- Bring a large pot 2/3 full of salted water to a boil over high heat.
- Add pasta and cook, stirring occasionally until *al dente*.
- Drain pasta.
- Put linguine in 6 serving dishes.
- Pour artichoke sauce (enough to combine with pasta) and toss to mix.
- Spoon shrimp on top of each serving dish.
- Serve grated cheese on the side, so each person can help themselves according to their taste.

Chocolate Mousse Pie

I like to serve a fabulous elegant dessert to top off dinner, plus a berry or fruit bowl for people to have as another choice. I might also put a dish of good quality chocolate mints on the table. This dessert can be prepared in advance and frozen. If frozen, thaw overnight in refrigerator. Or, make in advance on the day of your party. This dessert always gets raves. It is yummy.

Crust

Ingredients:
- 3 cups chocolate wafer crumbs
- 1/2 cup (1 stick) unsalted butter melted

Method:
- Combine crumbs and butter.
- Press on bottom and completely up sides of 10-inch spring form pan.
- Refrigerate for 30 minutes, or chill in freezer.

Filling

Ingredients:
- 1 pound semi-sweet chocolate; buy gourmet
- 2 eggs
- 4 egg yolks
- 2 cups whipping cream
- 6 tablespoons powdered sugar
- 4 egg whites, room temperature

Method:
- Soften chocolate in top of double boiler over simmering water.
- Let chocolate cool to lukewarm.
- Add whole eggs and mix well.
- Add yolks and mix until thoroughly blended.
- Whip cream with powdered sugar until soft peaks form.
- Beat egg whites until stiff, but not dry.
- Stir a little of the cream and whites gently, until incorporated completely.
- Turn mixture into crust.
- Chill at least 6 hours, or preferably overnight.
- When pie is chilled, whip remaining 2 cups of cream with powdered sugar to taste, until quite stiff.
- Loosen crust on all sides using a sharp knife, remove spring form.
- Spread cream on top of the mousse.

*Within each of us lies a wellspring of
abundance and the seeds of opportunity.
For each of us there is a deeply personal dream
waiting to be discovered and fulfilled.
When we cherish our dream and then invest love,
creative energy, perseverance, and passion in ourselves,
we will achieve an authentic success.*

Sara Ban Breathnach

Maggie Martin

Alexandria, LA

If you have made mistakes there is always another chance for you ...you may have a fresh start any moment you choose, for this thing we call 'failure' is not the falling down, but the staying down.

Mary Pickford

Maggie Martin

Mrs. Jonathan Martin, 1971

Mothers and Daughters, 1981, left to right:
Me, Natalie, Amanda and my mom, Vivian

Where does one start when instructed to write a 'short biography?' Since any life writing begins at birth, mine necessarily begins in Etoile, Texas, where I lived my first 17 years. The French word for 'star,' Etoile has no foreign heritage. It is decidedly Southern in region, unequivocally East Texas in culture. In 1884, when its founding fathers selected the name Star for their post office, they learned another Texas town already had that name. Perhaps stubbornly determined to live in Star, they chose the French spelling. If 'star' is defined by its usual qualities—luminous, visible, superior—this small, rural community in the piney woods of deep East Texas may not live up to its French name. However, if 'star' (as the Star of Bethlehem) contributes to one's destiny, then, at least for me, Etoile did live up to its name.

Specifically, my hometown fashioned my person and personality. In this small community where God and family were the cornerstone of existence, I grew up with a strong belief that I was not alone in my journey through life. Even in moments of solitude, I felt the personal presence of Another. The resulting sense of empowerment was palpable, even for a 17-year-old who left for college with a dream in her pocket.

My beautiful family – left to right: Johnny, Amanda, me, Natalie, 2000

Traveling in Paris, France with my husband, Johnny, 1999

Basically, my dream was to succeed, to do well at something or some things, to make a difference, to touch some lives along the way, to love and to be loved. This may seem like an impossible, all-inclusive dream, but I daresay it is not unlike the one envisioned by others who go out into the world for the first time.

Did I succeed in my dream? Infinitely greater than I could have imagined. In 1989, after graduating with a

degree in English from Sam Houston State University in Huntsville, Texas, I enrolled at Louisiana State University in Baton Rouge, Louisiana, for a graduate degree. I planned to spend two years in Louisiana, returning to Texas to work toward a third degree. However, as often happens, my plans took an unexpected detour. That detour came through a person, my husband of 30 years–Jonathan Martin.

We married in June 1971, setting up housekeeping in Ringgold, Louisiana, a small town not much larger than Etoile. I had sworn I would never again live in a rural area! What did our moms tell us when we were growing up? "Never say never." Our ten years in Ringgold were years of adjustment (to marriage, to life without a university and a continued education), of thankfulness (for surviving a near-fatal automobile accident in 1972, for having a caring husband in this unexpected time of difficulty), and of indescribable joy (in giving birth to a beautiful daughter Natalie in 1976 and to another equally beautiful daughter Amanda in 1980).

Having our daughters and raising them in a Christian home became my priority for the next several years. What greater success exists than to, at least in part, shape two small beings into self-sufficient individuals who can claim their own dreams for success? Truly my greatest legacy, both are now well on the way toward their personal successes. A graduate of Vanderbilt University, Natalie is an environmental engineer working in Baton Rouge. She recently completed her MBA at Louisiana State University. Regardless of the task placed before her, Natalie excels, the sign of a leader in the making.

Amanda graduated with a degree from Vanderbilt's Blair School of Music. A consummate entertainer on stage (our own diva) and with a strong sense of self and commitment to Christ, she spreads a bit of 'star' dust wherever she goes. (Perhaps a bit of latent 'Etoile power' is at work in her.) Amanda is preparing now to further her musical education. One day we will proudly attend one of her performances in New York or Europe.

In 1981, our family moved to Alexandria, Louisiana, headquarters for Johnny's family business, Roy O. Martin Lumber Company. An exciting move, it provided additional opportunities for all of us. Johnny began growing the company with construction of an Oriented Strand Board plant in 1983, a hardwood

Dr. Maggie Martin, 1995

sawmill in 1984, and a plywood plant in 1996. Alexandria gave Natalie and Amanda opportunities to meet new friends, to find ways to express their talents, and to learn their worlds are limited only by their imaginations. And, it placed me near Louisiana College, a small liberal arts college where, in 1985, I returned to academia.

After teaching part-time for five years, I decided to reach for my deferred dream of that third degree. Still teaching in 1990, and with the encouragement of a supportive husband, I began a two-hour commute twice weekly to LSU in Baton Rouge. Five years later, I fulfilled the dream I had first envisioned in the late 1960's, but the one I now jokingly called my 'mid-life crisis': a Doctorate of Philosophy, or Ph.D.

Because writing my dissertation required an inordinate amount of time, research and concentration, I quit teaching in 1993, fully intending to return to academia when I completed my degree. Again, though, my life detoured. This detour was the creation of Rhetorlnc, Inc., my writing consulting business. Through discussions with Johnny, I had become aware of the need for raising basic writing skills among those in the business world.

The personal computer and e-mail have drastically changed the landscape of business writing during the past 20 years. Twenty years ago, only a few executives and upper-level managers regularly wrote letters. Even if their correctness skills were lacking, they generally had secretaries who could catch and correct errors. Today, though, many in the workplace write and send numerous documents daily. Unfortunately, many of today's business writers have neither the skills necessary for successful business writing, nor the luxury of secretaries to proof their writing.

Realizing this niche, I developed a writing seminar to take into interested businesses. In a two-day seminar, I cannot teach everything one needs to know about business writing. However, I can raise an awareness of the need to communicate correctly. Additionally, I can provide resource materials for participants to use to improve their writing skills and inspiration to assure them that writing correctly can be learned—even for an adult.

I firmly believe that we are gifted to reach our highest potential, whether it is as simple as learning to write correctly or as complex as making a difference in the world around us. All we have to do is put forth the effort and claim the dream, that 'deeply personal dream waiting to be discovered and fulfilled.' And, no, fulfilling a dream is neither quick nor easy. Like my Ph.D., a dream may be deferred 25 years or even longer. "But if we cherish our dream and then invest love, creative energy, perseverance, and passion in ourselves, we will achieve [our] authentic success." — Breathnach

Maggie B. Martin

Celebrating Christmas, 2000

Dinner with Goddess Maggie

Maggie's Menu

When Johnny and I entertain, we usually invite at least three couples, making a dinner party for eight. Our dining table easily seats that number, and I find it as easy to prepare for eight guests as it is to prepare for four. Thus, each of my recipes provides ample servings for eight. If you serve fewer than eight, don't panic. Prepare each recipe as instructed, and you'll have enough left over for another day!

My dinner offering is quite flexible. You can make it a formal dinner event with candles, fine china and linens, as we frequently do in the dining room. Or, you can make it a casual dining experience, buffet style. Generally, I serve buffet style, even in the more formal setting. In so doing, each guest can choose individual portion sizes.

Recently I added a creative new 'wrinkle' to a dinner party. It worked so well that I will regularly incorporate it into my entertaining. I set each place with one of four pair of Waterford toasting flutes, purposely placing the matching pairs apart from each other. At dinnertime, I instructed our female guests to select their places. To encourage interaction among our guests, I then instructed the male spouses to find the flute that matched their mate's. After everyone located their correct places, which might have been adjacent to a new acquaintance, we then each made a pre-dinner toast that was appropriate to the flute (happiness, prosperity, love or health). The surprise was that each flute amazingly related to the particular situations of all our guests at that point in their lives!

- Crab Appetizer
- Cakebread Chardonnay
- Rosemount Estate Shiraz
- Green and Orange Salad
- Green Bean Bundles
- Grilled Beef Tenderloin
- Sourdough Bread
- Mom's 'Best-Ever' Apple Pie
- Coffee

notes:

Crab Appetizer

This appetizer is oh-so-easy. Everyone who tastes it loves it and wants the recipe! Be prepared to share it. The red chili sauce topping creates an especially pretty dish, perfect for all occasions.

Ingredients:
- 1 (12) ounce pkg. cream cheese, softened
- 1/2 onion, grated
- 2 tablespoons Worcestershire sauce
- dash of garlic salt
- 1 tablespoon lemon juice
- 1 (6) ounce can crabmeat
- 2 tablespoons mayonnaise

Method:
- Mix all and form into a ball on serving dish.

Topping Ingredients:
- 6 ounces chili sauce
- 1 tablespoon horseradish

Topping Method:
- Mix and pour over crab ball.
- Serve with wheat crackers or Fritos.

notes:

notes:

Green and Orange Salad

This is another very easy dish to prepare. You can make the dressing days ahead and keep it in the refrigerator. In fact, if you are cooking only for two (as I now do most of the time), you can use only as much dressing as you need. You can also be creative by adding grilled chicken, making this salad a delicious main dish.

Ingredients:
- Romaine lettuce, one pound
- 2 cans mandarin oranges, drained
- 4 ounces slivered almonds. Toast the almonds at 250° for 20 minutes.

Dressing Ingredients:
- 1/2 cup canola oil
- 1 teaspoon celery seed
- 1/3 cup red wine vinegar
- 1 teaspoon salt
- 2/3 cup white sugar
- dash fresh-ground pepper
- 3 teaspoons yellow mustard
- dash onion salt

Method:
- Mix dressing ingredients and refrigerate overnight.
- Before serving, pour oranges, almonds and dressing over romaine, or other leafy lettuce.

Green Bean Bundles

This recipe should serve 6–8 adults. However, if you have hearty eaters you may want to double the recipe for eight adults, since most come back for second helpings. If you're in a hurry and don't have time to wrap the beans in bacon, you can take my shortcut. Cut the bacon in small pieces and mix with the loose beans. They're just as tasty, albeit not quite as impressive looking.

Ingredients:
- 4 cans vertical-packed green beans
- 8 slices bacon

Marinade Ingredients:
- 1/2 cup brown sugar
- 1/2 cup melted butter (not margarine)
- 1/2 teaspoon garlic salt
- dash of soy sauce

Method:
- Cut bacon in half; take 9–10 beans and wrap with bacon.
  (If necessary, secure with toothpicks.)
- Place bundles in a 9"x13" pan.
- Cover with marinade and refrigerate overnight.
- Bake at 350° for 30 minutes.

notes:

notes:

Grilled Beef Tenderloin

So that you don't burn the outside of the tenderloin, cook on indirect heat for the first half of cooking. Then place on direct heat to sear the flavors.

10 pound beef tenderloin

Marinade Ingredients:
- 1/2 cup chopped onion
- 1/2 teaspoon pepper
- 1/2 cup lemon juice
- 1/2 teaspoon thyme, dried
- 1/4 cup salad oil
- 1/2 teaspoon oregano, dried
- 1/2 teaspoon salt
- 1/2 teaspoon rosemary, dried
- 1/2 teaspoon celery salt
- 2 cloves garlic, minced

Method:
- Combine all ingredients except the tenderloin.
- Place the tenderloin in a container that can be tightly sealed. Pour marinade over the tenderloin, marinating it in the refrigerator for 4–6 hours, or overnight. (The longer you marinate, the more tender and flavorful the meat will be.)
- Grill to the doneness you prefer.

Crisco Pie Crust

I've tried numerous pie crust recipes. This is by far the best one I've found. Once you learn how to handle the dough, you'll make deliciously flaky pie crust. For a single recipe, cut ingredients in half.

The secret to making a good pie crust is to handle the dough as little as possible. You don't knead pie dough the way you would knead bread dough. Rather, you simply mould the dough in your hands, just enough to hold it together for rolling out.

I find that a pastry 'sock' around the rolling pin and a pastry cloth for rolling the dough make the process almost error free. Otherwise, the dough tends to stick to the rolling pin and the counter top…a very frustrating experience.

notes:

notes:

Ingredients:
- 2 2/3 cups sifted regular flour
- 1 teaspoon salt
- 1 cup Crisco
- 6 tablespoons water
- 2 tablespoons butter, or margarine

Method:
- Sift flour before measuring; spoon lightly into measuring cup and level.
- Combine flour and salt in mixing bowl.
- With a pastry blender, cut in Crisco until uniform; mixture should be fairly coarse.
- Sprinkle with water, a tablespoon at a time; toss with a fork.
- Work dough into 2 firm balls with your hands.
- Set aside one pastry ball for top crust.
- Press 1 ball of dough into a flat circle with smooth edges.
- On a lightly floured surface, roll dough to a circle about 1 1/2 inches larger than inverted pie plate.
- Gently ease dough onto pie plate. (Sometimes it helps if you gently fold over the crust to put it into the plate. Then it doesn't break so easily. Unfold it after getting it into the plate.)
- Trim 1/2 inch beyond outside edge of plate.
- Set aside as you prepare filling.

Mom's 'Best-Ever' Apple Pie

This pie requires a bit of effort. Since I first made this pie as a bride, it has been the favorite dessert of Johnny, my husband of thirty years. Most men especially like this dessert. Maybe it reminds each man of his mom's apple pie made with love. It certainly qualifies as a 'comfort food', especially when you serve it with a scoop of vanilla ice cream. I recommend Blue Bell ice cream, if you can purchase it in your area. I think the key ingredients are the raisins and pecans. Not only do they boost the flavor, but they also give a pleasantly surprising crunch to the taste.

Apple Filling Ingredients:
- 5 cups thinly sliced red Rome apples
- 1 teaspoon lemon juice
  (sprinkle lemon juice over apples)
- 1 cup sugar
- 2 tablespoons flour
- 1/2 teaspoon cinnamon
- 1/4 teaspoon nutmeg
- 1/4 teaspoon salt
- 1/4 cup raisins (optional)
  To soften raisins, soak in 1/2 cup warm water
- 1/4 cup finely chopped pecans (optional)

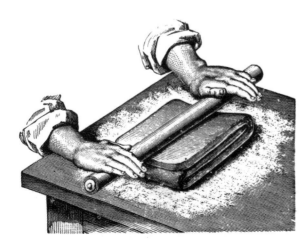

notes:

Method:
- Pre-heat oven to 375°–400°.
- Combine sugar, flour, spices, and salt.
- Add to apples.
- Add drained raisins and pecans to apple mixture; toss to mix.
- Add half the apples to crust in the pan; pack well. Dot with half of butter.
- Add remaining apples. Dot with remaining half of butter.
- Moisten rim of crust with water.
- Roll out top crust. Cut vents near center. Adjust top crust. Leave about 1/2" pastry beyond edge; fold it over the bottom layer of pastry.
- Seal rim by pressing together; flute edges.
- Brush with milk.
- If desired, sprinkle top with cinnamon and sugar mixture.
- Bake for 50–60 minutes, or until apples test done with fork.

*We all live in suspense, from day to day,
from hour to hour, in other words
we are the hero of our own story.*

Mary McCarthy

Mary Ann Grant

San Francisco, CA

*A woman's life can really
be a succession of lives, each
revolving around some emotionally
compelling situation or challenge,
and each marked off by some
intense experience.*

Wallis, Duchess of Windsor

Mary Ann Grant

Blessing my Hawaiian name — Kahanu 'okalani, breath of heaven' —Honolulu, early 1990's

Happy childhood, 4 years old, San Francisco, 1946

I grew up in a traditional home in the San Francisco Bay Area. My expectation and belief was that life would echo that of my parents. I would marry a successful businessman, raise a family and live happily ever after. Instead, I graduated from a finishing/modeling school, married young, attended college and had a short modeling career. Boy, was I in for a surprise! My life wasn't anything like my parents, falling short of the Cinderella dream I had been raised to believe would be mine.

The first turning point in my life, and perhaps the most significant, was the birth of my first-born son and the first grandchild in our family. David quickly became the joy of us all. His life unfolded as expected until he was around the age of two, when I noticed something was wrong. After specialists' examinations and numerous tests, we discovered that the necessary surgery he had at three weeks old had shocked his central nervous system, causing him developmental disabilities.

Nearly 40 years ago, special education was in its yearling stages, and I was told there was no way for my son to attend school. Even though I was young, naïve and shy, I wouldn't take no for an answer. With the help of my father, we arranged for a meeting with the superintendent of schools to discuss David's educational needs. The power of one parent, with a burning desire, can create a miracle. Within a month we had a teacher, a classroom and seven other children attending school with my son. This was an educational first. A grandmother, who was raising her grandchild, called me one day to thank me for making it possible for her grandson to finally attend school. Her grandson was nine years old.

Raising a special child, when professionals knew so little and with few educational avenues available, became a daunting task. In addition to David, who was then seven, I had two younger children, my second son Paul and daughter Gina, who also needed me. My journey with David took me into many places and realms that I had no knowledge of, or ever thought I would investigate. Painful experiences were abundant and reached to the very depth of my being. The greatest gifts David has given me are incredible self-discovery and internal strength, allowing me to develop courage and compassion.

Special Events Director for Liberty House, Honolulu, early 1990's

Many years were spent raising the children as a single parent. My first career effort to financially support my family was as a director for the finishing school from which I'd graduated. The hard work and struggles as a single parent were many. What I learned was dedication and determination, setting in motion an unforgettable life journey.

Years later I remarried. Just when I thought all was going well, my husband of six years decided to go it alone. Once again, I had tried to have the traditional marriage, staying home to raise my children through their teen years. By this time two of the children were in college, and my special son settled in an independent living/working program in a small community near our home. My goal was for him to be independent, enabling him to handle life long after I am gone.

My treasured children – left to right: Gina, Paul, David, Mother's Day 2000

After an absence of several years from the job market, I found myself alone. Once again, I was starting over. An interview with a local public television station led to a job being created for me as the special projects manager. Several years later, I received a phone call that would dramatically change my life…again. An executive recruiter at the largest retail department store in Honolulu, Hawaii, asked me to consider a position. I was thrilled and excited about the prospect of a new adventure.

The move to Hawaii was heart wrenching and difficult, knowing I would be leaving my children, although they were now all independent young adults. I moved to Hawaii not knowing anyone, except my future boss. For the first time in my life, I was away from family and close friends. The lessons were many— learning to pronounce the Hawaiian names of streets, interacting with a multiplicity of cultures, making new friends, and learning a new job. I had a successful and enriching career in retail. I was at the top of my game with the responsibility of directing special events for eleven stores. I was able to stretch my creative abilities in a large arena.

Of most importance was how I transformed in the fifteen years of living in the magical and spiritual islands of Hawaii. Living on an island, surrounded by the 'emotional' body of water, became the best and most sacred experience of my life so far. I embraced the island style and the people with all my heart. This heart energy was returned to me a thousand times over. The 'Aloha Spirit' of the island people expanded my inner-self, opening my heart like never before. Living where the beauty is so exquisite has made me grateful, learning how little I need. I will always cherish the sights of sunrises and sunsets, the sounds of rolling surf and gentle trade winds, soft air fragrant with the scent of flowers and brilliant rainbows. Each and every island, unique in its own way, offers magnificent beauty.

My precious grandchildren – left to right: Abigail (3), Anna (7 months), and Jeremiah (2), 2001

One of the most divinely inspired and sacred times for me was meeting a Hawaiian chief and telling him of a dream I had about the Goddess Pele. He knew how much I loved the islands and the aina (land). He said it was time for me to be given a Hawaiian name, something one cannot ask for. I was humbled and thrilled by this unique gift. There was a ceremony at a church in Honolulu, blessing my new name by a Hawaiian Minister. I will always consider this blessing an honor.

Relaxing in Atlanta, 2001

After living in paradise for fifteen years, another road is before me now. I face another transition, having moved back to the mainland to start a new life. Once again, I am heading in a new direction with a career path yet to unfold. This time I will be surrounded by my children and grandchildren, and whomever else I am meant to meet along my journey homeward.

Mary Ann Grant

Dinner with Goddess Mary Ann

I adapted this menu from my Italian roots, adding an American style. It is simple to prepare and gets great reviews. The main dish is Manzo Vapore with potatoes, vegetables and a salad, served all at once or family style. However, having dinner with a goddess, in my opinion, should be long and leisurely. There should be plenty of time to enjoy dining and good conversation. Therefore, I have planned the meal in courses.

The kitchen was the heart center in my family where everyone, including the men, gathered to talk. Our social life was centered on food, spending hours around the dining table laughing and talking. Italian passion was rampant, yet everyone went home with hugs and kisses. When my family got together for a holiday or celebration, the tables were abundant with different and delectable regional dishes. When Nonna (grandmother in Italian) and my aunties visited, my senses were filled with the smells of garlic and onions simmering on the stove, as they started preparing spaghetti sauce along with the morning coffee. The sauce would simmer for hours, in time for lunch or the evening meal. All the women in my family taught me cooking skills as they shared their recipes. I learned needlework, as they told stories about child rearing or gave domestic tips, discussing what it meant to be a wife and mother.

When dining, I consider color and texture in the overall visual presentation. The color and style of your china creates a background, showcasing the colors and texture of the food. Colors and texture can be picked up in the linens and with a centerpiece for the table. Since this is a country meal, a simple arrangement of fall leaves or herbs (what you might have growing in your garden) could be used. I love candles, but keep them burning low, adding a warm glow without distraction. I love Italian music playing in the background while I sip a glass of wine. It sets the mood and adds to my pleasure of creation.

And what would an Italian meal be without wine? Chardonnay or one of your favorite white wines would complement the appetizer and salad. A Pinot Noir, Merlot or Cabernet would go nicely with the main entrée. If you're really in a festive mood, serve Frangelico or Amaretto liqueur with dessert. *Buon appetito!*

Mary Ann's Menu

- Melon Wrapped with Proscuitto
- Mixed Greens Salad
- Manzo Vapore
- Mashed Potatoes and Vegetables
- Italian Custard
- Coffee
- Dessert Liqueur (optional)

notes:

Proscuitto and Melon

This is a very easy appetizer, offering a tasty beginning to your meal. Proscuitto di Parma is a fragrant and sweet ham produced in a specifically designated area, in the province of Parma, Italy. It is easily available at any shop that imports fine Italian foods. Taste a sample before buying. It should have the sweet flavor of a young and tender ham, not salty.

Ingredients:
- 1 large ripe cantaloupe or two small ones
- 6 slices of Proscuitto di Parma

Method:
- Cut melon in half and remove rind and seeds.
- Cut each half into three wedges.
- Take the Proscuitto and wrap around melon.
- Place on a serving dish or individual plates.

Salad of Baby Greens

Ingredients:
- 1 small head each of romaine, radicchio, red-leaf lettuce and curly endive
- 1/2 cup of fresh basil leaves if desired
- 1/2 cup Kalamata olives
- 1 small red onion, sliced (soak in water to remove sharpness)
- 1/3 cup pine nuts (toasted)
- 2 to 3 ounces Parmigiano-Reggiano cheese shaved with a vegetable peeler into thin curls.
- 1/3 to 1/2 cup of extra-virgin olive oil
- 3 to 4 tablespoons of balsamic vinegar
- salt and ground pepper to taste

Method:
- Wash and dry the lettuces, discarding any bruised leaves.
- Break up into small bite-sized pieces.
- Wash and dry basil leaves. This can be done hours ahead of time and stored in plastic bags in the refrigerator to chill.
- Mix extra-virgin olive oil and balsamic vinegar together.
- Assemble all ingredients in a bowl. Toss with oil and vinegar, salt and pepper to taste.

Vegetable

Several vegetables could be used to accompany the entrée. Broccoli, string beans, spinach or red swiss chard are all good choices. Red swiss chard would be an attractive embellishment to the main dish, both in color and texture. I did not include a recipe for mashed potatoes, suspecting everyone knows how to make them.

Ingredients:
- 1 large bunch of red swiss chard
- 2 cloves of garlic
- 2 tablespoons extra-virgin olive oil and 2 tablespoons butter
- salt and pepper

Method:
- Wash and drain red swiss chard. Remove any bruised leaves and trim stalks.
- Use a steamer or put about I inch of water in a pot, bring to a boil and steam until tender.
- Remove and drain. If swiss chard leaves are large, cut into 2" strips vertically and horizontally to make nice bite-size pieces.
- Heat olive oil and butter in a pan over medium heat. Add sliced garlic and sauté for a few minutes, being careful not to burn the garlic.
- Add swiss chard and toss leaves. Salt and pepper to taste.
- Keep warm until serving.

Manzo Vapore

Manzo Vapore is a hearty winter meal. Nonna was a very good cook, representing a country style she learned from her mother. She came from a small town in the province of Bergamo in Northern Italy. As far as my mother knows, this recipe was Nonna's own creation. Meals were never formal, always delicious and simple to assemble. Her daughters, including my mother, learned to prepare meals each day for their family of nine. These recipes were never measured nor written down, but passed on from mother to daughter. To this day, I measure by sight.

Ingredients:
- 3 to 4 pounds blade pot roast or boneless chuck pot roast
- 2 tablespoons olive oil and 1 tablespoon butter or margarine
- 1 large onion studded with whole cloves (cover half of onion with cloves)
- salt and pepper
- cinnamon stick (broken in small pieces)
- 1 cup Burgundy wine
- 1 to 2 tablespoons cornstarch diluted with milk

Method:
- Heat olive oil and margarine in a large stockpot or dutch oven.
- Brown meat on all sides.
  Season with salt and pepper.
- Add wine and rest of ingredients.
- Reduce heat, cover and simmer slowly turning meat often. Cook for 2 1/2 to 3 hours or until tender. Add a little water if needed to prevent sticking.
- When meat is cooked, remove it from the pot and strain the gravy.
- Add cornstarch to thicken if desired. The gravy is divine and should be generously spooned over meat slices and mashed potatoes.

Italian Custard

This dessert was a favorite of my Aunt Mary's. For years she pleaded with her friend to give her the recipe. It was one of his mother's special recipes that he was reluctant to share. He did finally give it to Mary, who was kind enough to pass it on to my mother, who decided to share it with me. This dessert could easily be made a day ahead and refrigerated.

Ingredients:
- 5 large eggs
- 2 cups milk
- 1 1/2 cups sugar
- 1 shot whiskey
- 1 teaspoon vanilla
- 12 Amaretto cookies (crumbled)
- 2 tablespoons instant chocolate

Method:
- Use a 1-quart ring mold.
- Caramelize 1/2 cup sugar inside the mold by placing over burner on medium heat, coating the bottom and all sides of mold. Let cool.
- Mix all ingredients together; put into mold.
- Cover the mold with foil and place the mold into a dutch oven with 2 inches of water.
- Cover the dutch oven with a lid.
- After water comes to a boil, simmer 20 minutes.
- Remove mold from the dutch oven and chill custard for several hours.
- Invert on a plate before serving.

You can't change the music of your soul.

Katherine Hepburn

Mary Kay Doherty

Carson City, NV

*The most profound relationship
we'll ever have is the one
with ourselves.*

Shirley MacLaine

140

My siblings and me with our mother – Tonopah, NV 1955

Not quite 1 year old, 1944

I was born in October 1943 in Illinois, the eldest child of my father's second family. We numbered four, two girls and two boys. We began our lives in the outskirts of Chicago, living in a house with a backyard filled with swings, slides and a sandbox. We also had two donkeys named Susie and Sarah. Our donkeys were the cause of many nights' lost sleep by my mother, and any other unsuspecting visitor, as they were crafty and able to unlatch their corral fence.

The ending of World War II prompted a move to Nevada, where my father was to manage mining and mill start-up operations. I was nearing age eight and going into the third grade when we moved to the dusty desert town of Tonopah. Gold, silver and precious uranium for potentially making bombs attracted investors who hired my father as the front man in this very unpopulated place. Lawns and even trees were seldom found. But the raised sidewalks, hitching posts for horses, and especially our introduction to real Indians excited the four of us children, and we hardly missed the verdant Midwest of our birth.

Another first for the four of us was Tonopah's old wooden movie house. The movies were changed weekly. Since most movies of that day were tame enough, we generally went each Friday evening. However, we all four agreed, no actors were more glamorous than our own momma and daddy. Somewhere along the way my father was gifted with a wine colored smoking jacket that made him look dapper. I remember fondly watching our mother dressing up for Saturday night 'dates'; or, my parents dressing formal, heading off to a dance sponsored by the Odd Fellows or Eastern Star Ladies Organization. My first impressions when seeing the formal evening attire with long gloves, silver or gold shoes, and all the other finery, left me daydreaming of a time when I could go too.

At 16, the pre-mature death of my mother left me, my siblings and father devastated. That loss continues to impact me today. Our idyllic life was ended and nothing would ever be the same.

First goddess gathering with my daughter, Walterboro, SC 1990

My college graduation – left to right: Cahal, Kathleen. Me, 1982

Mother's death in 1960 will always be the most telling and compelling influence on my life. There is a continual feeling of incompletion, an ever-present feeling of uncertainty within. This natural link with my sense of womanhood was cut short, directly impacting my sense of self.

Lounging at home, Carson City, NV, 1995

It was in San Francisco that I met and fell in love with Cahal Doherty. He had recently moved to California after leaving Ireland. I believed him to be not only handsome but an Irish David Niven, an actor I had always admired. And I, like innumerable women of our era, rejoiced at my wedding; and then later, rejoiced at the magical and mysterious birth of my only child, Kathleen.

At 39, I graduated from a university with a BA degree. I began college at 19, taking nearly 20 years to keep this commitment of completing my degree. It remains my single greatest accomplishment beyond motherhood. Staying in the process of getting my degree is a testament of my willingness to hold onto a dream, and the tenacity to accomplish such a goal. I look to this achievement often because I sometimes feel adrift, like I am accomplishing little or getting nowhere fast. I am searching for a dream again, something to give me direction, still wondering what I will do when I grow up. Much of this internal searching feels tied to the passing of my mother early in my life.

Prior to mother's death, I lived with my paternal aunt in San Francisco. I was to be a junior in high school. It was determined that I should get additional Catholic education from the Presentation High School nuns, well-known and respected educators in the city. My aunt taught, and later became the director of nursing for St. Joseph's College of Nursing. She had been a constant visitor to our home no matter where we lived. Her educated Victorian grace instilled us with love and awe. Her leadership and constant strength were a major influence, as we floundered in the immediate months of mourning. She ultimately paid for my high school years, as well as those for my sister. Aunt Madeleine mentored all four of us children, introducing us to the arts, museums and theatre. She is the most unforgettable character in my life script.

I know that all life has meaning and I long to go about it purposefully. Yet, just the day-to-day existence such as getting on with everyday chores, seems to be more the flow of my days. Rarely do I have a clear internal map of where I am heading. Thus, when I was invited to contribute to the 'goddess' book, I was delighted. Here was something to which I could contribute, while being socially involved with a number of beloved and honorable women. Reflecting on food and entertaining, both dear to my heart, gave me a focus. It was fun pouring over recipes and putting together my menu. Entertaining is something I have always loved to do.

My husband, Cahal and me at our nephew's wedding, 1998

I have learned that something I do with joy and much love, something that is natural to me, is where I am truly myself. That perhaps being 'grown up' is becoming so aware of oneself, it then becomes easy to spend most of one's days doing what gives one joy. I believe love is always the highest expression. The opportunity to feel life as precious and full of wonder may be the true reason for how we spend our days. I see myself as an ordinary woman who has known extraordinary influences. I am a woman who still dreams of being seen in all my magnificence.

Mary Kay Hines-Doherty

The process of putting together my contribution for the book caused some real soul searching. Creating a short biography has been much more challenging than anticipated. I was uncertain how to present myself because it was uncomfortable to take myself seriously. I came face-to-face with the fears and losses of my childhood. My uncertainty at being worthy surfaced as many questions passed through my mind: Will I be accepted, liked, admired? Will I be worthy of this spotlight? Will I shine? I suddenly realized that I have always taken myself very seriously, but am nearly paralyzed if another person does too.

Dinner with Goddess Mary Kay

Mary Kay's Menu

- White Gazpacho Soup
- Baked Chicken Divan
- Long Grain White Rice
- Avocado and Tomato Salad
  with Champagne Dressing
- Crescent Rolls
- Wine
- Raspberry Sorbet with Fresh
  Berries and Chocolate Sauce
- Coffee

notes:

I always feel happy and joyful when preparing a meal for those I love. I love everything about the process from deciding on the menu, to food shopping, to preparation, to serving my guests. This is a way that I create. I've been told that when I'm in the kitchen I'm my most relaxed, flowing self. Cooking in my kitchen literally makes me sing. There is nothing better for my soul than creating a meal for those I love.

The main dish I selected is an elegant casserole introduced in the 1950's, and it endures and satisfies into the new millennium. Both the Gazpacho Soup and the Chicken Divan can be made a day ahead, enhancing the flavors and making elegant entertaining easy. The wine I recommend is either a Green Hungarian or a Chenin Blanc. I've created a dinner for eight. Please enjoy.

White Gazpacho Soup

This soup can be prepared the day before. Just before serving, blend again. A few bits of chopped tomato on top are a nice garnish.

Ingredients:
- 4 cucumbers
- 2 (14.5) ounce cans of chicken broth
- 2 cups sour cream
- 1 clove garlic
- 4 tablespoons rice vinegar
- 2 tablespoons salt

Method:
- Peel and seed cucumber, then slice.
- Mince garlic in blender.
- Add cucumber and blend.
- Add vinegar and salt, then purée till smooth.
- Add sour cream and 1/2 of broth, and then blend.
- Add remaining broth and blend.
- Chill.

notes:

Chicken Divan

Ingredients:
- 8 boneless/skinless chicken breasts
- 2 or 3 chicken bouillon cubes
- 2 (14.5) cans ounce cream of chicken soup
- 1 1/2 cups mayonnaise
- 1 teaspoon lemon juice
- 2 boxes frozen broccoli or asparagus. (If using fresh, you'll need enough to layer your casserole completely.)
- 1 or 2 cups of grated sharp cheddar cheese
- 1 cup fresh or packaged plain bread crumbs

Method:
- Pre-heat oven to 350°.
- Using a deep-sided pan, poach chicken breasts, using enough water to cover completely. Add bouillon to the water for extra flavor. This process will take about 15 minutes, or until white throughout. Let cool.
- As the chicken is poaching, combine undiluted soup, mayonnaise and lemon juice, then set aside.
- Steam frozen or fresh broccoli or asparagus till just done.
- Grate the cheese and measure out breadcrumbs.
- Lightly cover casserole dish with mayonnaise to prevent sticking.
- Begin layering, first pulling cooked chicken into large bite-size bits, using half of the chicken.
- Add the vegetables, in bite sizes too. Use only half.
- Add the grated cheese. Again, save some for the top of your dish.
- Then repeat these last three steps again, using the remainder of your ingredients.
- Finally, when the layering is done, sprinkle on the breadcrumbs.
- Bake for 30 minutes or so, until bubbling throughout.

Long Grain White Rice

Cook as directed, adding 1 chicken bouillon cube per cup of water.

Avocado and Tomato Salad

Ingredients:
- 3 ripe, but still firm, avocados
- 6 ripe, but still firm, tomatoes

Method:
- Slice and dice both vegetables and place in a serving bowl.
- Drizzle dressing over your salad and toss gently. I recommend Girard's Champagne Dressing, purchased at your local market.

notes:

notes:

Dessert

Ingredients:
- 2 containers Häagen-Dazs Raspberry Sorbet
- 1 package fresh or frozen raspberries
- 1 bottle chocolate sauce

Method:
- Dish up sorbet into your favorite dessert dishes.
- Spoon over fresh or thawed raspberries.
- Drizzle with chocolate sauce for those who want it.

Selfishness is not living as one wishes to live,

it is asking others to live as one wishes to live.

Ruth Rendell

Pamela Daniele

Atlanta, GA

*The especial genius of women,
I believe, is electrical in
movement, intuitive in
function, spiritual in tendency.*

Margaret Fuller

149

Pamela Daniele

Sweet Sixteen
San Mateo, CA, 1960

My dear family and me – left to right:
Grandma Margaret, Grandpa George,
me and my mother, Eve, 1952

At 3 years, in the outfit grandma made, 1947

I was born in San Francisco in 1944, growing up in the golden era of California during the post-war period. My early years were carefree and full of joy. My family lived in a neighborhood where I could safely roam free, running through the field behind our house and climbing majestic Eucalyptus trees. In the early evening hours I would play outside games with the many kids in my neighborhood, before racing home to a family dinner. I felt comfortable in my body, being naturally athletic. I engaged life with little fear, feeling I could do most anything.

Then came adolescence. Everything seemed to change during my teen years. Suddenly it felt as if I were in a foreign land. It was no longer acceptable for me to play sports with the boys. So now where did I fit in? I still wanted to play basketball and flag football, yet all my girlfriends had moved on to flirting with the same boys that used to pick me for their teams. I was expected to go from competitive to compliant, from teammate to girlfriend. Fitting in with my friends became a challenge, even where previously I had never worried about being accepted. I felt as if I were being asked to compromise myself in order to have friends.

Sitting in indian cave dwelling, Bandelier National Monument, NM, 1998

I eventually got my bearings, participating in school plays, cheering at high school games as a pom-pom girl, dabbling in puppy love and dreaming of romance. I read magazines about Hollywood movie stars that influenced me, while listening to Frank Sinatra and Johnny Mathis croon about love. The 1950's were a blend of traditional values and Rock n' Roll bumping up against one another. I realized that dating involved a ritual of assessing one's value to the opposite sex, with looks being the greatest asset. I found it difficult to balance my desire for clarity and directness with socially appropriate responses.

I knew early on that I was not drawn to the traditional roles of wife and mother, so I decided a business career would suit me best. First I needed to get my bearings in the outside world, which meant doing something that felt like being a part of a team. With this in mind, I completed a BA degree in Public Relations. The business world afforded me the opportunity to use many of my skills and talents. In business I could try on different aspects of myself, a launching pad for the adult interpersonal skills I've developed over the years. Working in a corporate setting expanded my mental agility and strength of character, while testing my intuition and heart. I learned courage, commitment, determination and perseverance.

I co-created a successful company that merged in 1998 with a public company, affording me the luxury of leaving the working world to ponder my next cycle of experience. Hollis, my business partner in that company and my best friend in life, became my husband. He stayed on with the merged company for a time, before electing to move on as a consultant representing our newest corporate creation. We continue to dialogue about how our newest business venture will move into the world, and what kind of offerings it will make in support of others. My relationship with Hollis has been an exquisite gift, giving me the space to deepen as a woman in the safety of a sweet and honoring love.

The past three years of my life have been about finding my passion again. The years of being the chief operating officer in a faced-paced high tech corporation left me feeling burned out and disconnected from my deeper sense of things. I began searching for what mattered to me at the heart level. During this inner journey of self-reflection and re-discovery of where I feel passion, I learned to appreciate cooking. This is the process that led to the vision for *Dinner With A Goddess*. The women in my life came through for me, sharing their tried and true recipes and teaching me the tricks of how to prepare easy yet yummy meals. Thanks to their friendship and guidance, I have learned to prepare healthy meals with minimum effort and maximum taste.

My second father, Ben, with me in Atlanta, 1999

Celebrating with my beloved husband, Hollis, 2001

My life-long quest for Spirit has led me down many rich and varied paths. In the 1960's, I was blessed with a mother who took me to lectures at Stanford University to learn about Kirlian photography. This process demonstrates that plants have a radiant energy field that responds to the touch of a hand or the tone of a voice. During that same time, Linus Pauling spoke at Standford on his theories of Vitamin C therapy and how we could heal ourselves. In the 1970's, Steven Halpern introduced a new kind of vibrational music using calibrated tones as healing frequencies, further influencing my studies in other non-traditional healing modalities.

In the early 1980's, I became certified in Polarity Therapy, doing this electro-magnetic energy work for about six years. The one constant through all my metaphysical studies has been the determination to stay true to my self.

A consistent theme in my life has been my on-going desire for deep and meaningful relationships. My life has been blessed with many unique women, who have become dear friends. Through many glorious moments of sharing dreams and desires, I've learned to cherish women deeply. In 1990, I began a tradition of holding 'goddess gatherings,' creating space for women to celebrate our authentic selves.

My sister goddesses have been invaluable in the discovery and recovery of my authentic self, gleaning greater value in all aspects of my life. These women have helped me learn to love in more expansive, less judgmental ways.

Pamela Daniele

You can contact Pamela at
www.unitygrid.com

Pamela's Menu

- California Sushi Rolls
- Gourmet Cheese & Crackers
- Wine
- Baby Bib Lettuce and Basil Salad
  with Vinaigrette Dressing
- Baked Salmon Supreme
- Mahatma Brown Rice
- Sautéed Asparagus with Walnuts
- Rum Cake
- Coffee and Tea

notes:

Dinner with Goddess Pamela

My style in life is casual. Because of this, I usually serve my meals restaurant style with the main portion of the meal served on the plate. I place the salad on the table so people can serve themselves. I allow myself much spontaneity in how I entertain, depending on who is coming to dinner. Selecting a meal that allows me time to be with my guests is what makes be happy.

This meal will take 45 minutes to prepare and serves six. The timing is based on how long the brown rice needs to cook. It does not include appetizer or dessert preparation, which can be done the day before or purchased from your local gourmet grocery. Somewhere along the way you've set your table, deciding what kind of candles, flowers and music you will use to set the mood of your celebration. Pull out your favorite serving dishes and let your flair for presentation shine.

Wines I recommend would be either an oily, fruity Chardonnay such as Schafer Red Shoulder Ranch, or Coppola Diamond Series. If your guests prefer red, offer a velvety Pinot Noir such as Domaine Drouhin from the Willamette Valley in Oregon.

It is with great love that I offer you this simple fare. Experience has shown that I can maintain my weight, health and vitality more effortlessly if I prepare balanced nutritious meals with my own heart and hands.

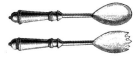

Baby Bib Lettuce and Basil Salad

I often use a pre-packaged, pre-washed organic baby bib lettuce salad mixture from Earthbound Farm, purchased in the local supermarket. This makes preparation very easy. If buying whole lettuce, I usually pre-cut all salad fixings and put in baggies earlier in the day, creating effortless assembly at party time. Your vinaigrette dressing can be prepared earlier ,too, adding more of anything to fit your taste.

Salad Ingredients:
- 2 pkgs. of Earthbound Farm Baby Bib lettuce or 2 heads of Red Leaf Boston lettuce, or the lettuce of your choice. Tear lettuce into bite-size pieces.
- 2 green onions (scallions), both the white and the greens parts, sliced
- 1 yellow and/or orange bell pepper, sliced julienne
- 12 leaves fresh basil, sliced julienne
- ranch flavored croutons, optional

Vinaigrette Ingredients:
- 1/4 cup extra virgin olive oil
- 2 tablespoons white balsamic vinegar
- salt and pepper to taste (It tastes better with freshly ground pepper.)

Salad Method:
- Mix all ingredients, except lettuce, together in bowl.
- Add vinaigrette dressing and toss thoroughly.
- Right before you serve your meal, add lettuce and coat the leaves lightly, so they don't get bruised or wilted.
- Serve either family style in one bowl or use individual plates.

Baked Salmon Supreme

The use of mayonnaise on salmon is a trick I learned from a friend who lives in the northwest (salmon country). It was a surprise to me that it tasted so good. It keeps the salmon very moist and flaky. I then added a little cayenne to give it a boost, and sprinkled paprika to give it a colorful, tasty topping. The dill adds the final touch, giving this dish a delightful flavor. I learned 'the parchment paper liner in tinfoil' trick from Goddess Vickie's offering in the book.

Ingredients:
- 6 salmon steaks, at least 2 1/2 inches wide, with bottom skin removed.
- 6 sheets of parchment paper from your local market.
- 6 sheets of aluminum foil the size of your parchment.
- 3 lemons, 1/2 lemon for each steak.
- 6 tablespoons light mayonnaise, 1 tablespoon for each steak.
- cayenne pepper.
- paprika.
- fresh dill.

Method:
- Pre-heat oven to 425°.
- Place each salmon steak in the center of a piece of aluminum foil that has been lined with parchment.
- Squeeze fresh lemon over each steak.
- Coat the top of each steak with mayonnaise
- Lightly dust each steak with cayenne pepper
- Sprinkle paprika liberally over the entire top of each piece
- Lay fresh dill sprigs over the top of each piece.
- Lift the sides of the aluminum foil and seal the top. Seal the ends.
- Bake for 25 minutes.
- Open each foil pouch and lift out fish with a spatula onto the individual plates
- Remove cooked dill, adding a fresh sprig before serving

Mahatma Brown Rice

The rice has the longest cooking time at around 40–45 minutes, so start this first. I add olive oil to the water because it brings out a nutty flavor in the rice. You'll probably have leftovers, which can be easily sautéed with veggies for another meal.

Ingredients:
- 2 cups Mahatma brown rice
- 4 cups water
- 2 teaspoons extra light olive oil, optional
- salt to taste

Method:
- Follow the cooking instructions on the rice package.
- Add salt and olive oil in the water before it boils, then add rice.

notes:

notes:

Sautéed Asparagus with Walnuts

Ingredients:
- 2 bundles fresh asparagus
- 2 to 4 tablespoons extra virgin olive oil
- 1 to 2 tablespoons minced garlic
- 1 cup chopped walnuts, optional
- 1 teaspoon mixed Italian herbs

Method:
- Wash and drain asparagus.
- Trim off the ends.
- Sauté all ingredients except for asparagus for 2 to 3 minutes.
- Add asparagus and continue sautéing for about 5 minutes, tossing often.
- Serve as soon as they are done.

Rum Cake

This recipe comes from my mother-in-law, Goddess Garland. Of all the great desserts she can create, this is my favorite. Once you begin to nibble on this treat, you will find it difficult to stop with just one slice. It will become a favorite for all occasions.

Ingredients:
- 1 yellow cake mix—Duncan Hines
- 1 vanilla instant pudding mix
- 4 eggs
- 1/3 cup canola oil
- 1/2 cup water
- 1/2 cup rum
- chopped nuts
- chopped cherries
- 1 non-stick bundt pan

Method:
- Pre-heat oven to 325°.
- Sprinkle chopped nuts and cherries in lightly floured bundt pan.
- Blend cake and pudding mixes.
- Add water, oil and rum.
- Beat in eggs one at a time.
- Pour batter into prepared pan and bake for 1 hour.

Sauce Ingredients:
- 1 margarine or butter
- 1/4 cup water
- 1 cup sugar
- 1/4 cup rum

Sauce Method:
- Combine all ingredients and bring to a boil.
- Boil 1 minute.
- Pour over cake while it is still in the pan as soon as it comes from the oven. Let set for 10 minutes.
- Make sure the sauce runs down the sides of the cake while in the pan. Use a regular dinner knife to separate sides from the pan to keep from scratching the non-stick coating of your bunt pan.
- Place plate on bottom of your pan and turn the cake over, gently lifting the bundt pan off the cake.
- If you have a glass cake cover, place over the plate to contain moisture and to keep fresh until serving.

*Living never wore one out
so much as the effort not to live.*

Anaïs Nin

Pola Reydburd

Miami Beach, FL

Life is either a daring
adventure or nothing.
Helen Keller

Pola Reydburd

Me with my son, Ilán, 10 days old, 1967

Showing off my dress, circa 1945

As it often happens on a ship, you look at people and try to imagine what they are like. Too Ritzy! Too Casual! Too Loud! Too Quiet! And then it dawns on you: These people seem just right! That's what my husband and I felt after meeting Hollis McNully and Pamela Daniele, during an exotic cruise to Oman, India, the Maldives and Thailand. We spent some time together, visiting ancient temples and bathing in the azure waters of the Indian Ocean. It was during our last day on board the ship we discovered that Pamela and I were both Aquarians; in fact just one day difference and one year difference. Somehow, that coincidence seemed to explain some of the empathy, the ease in communicating and the feeling of familiarity. It was as if we had known each other all our lives. We shared common interests, and Pamela and I in particular found that we had common concerns: Women's issues and community responsibility, to mention just two.

Having been brought up in a Jewish household (for many years, my grandparents were two of just a handful of people who kept a kosher home in Cali, Colombia), I was raised in a Catholic environment and attended a private Catholic school. My six Jewish classmates and I sang Christmas carols, participated in every extracurricular activity, and learned to protect our beliefs and respect our differences. The ability to preserve one's traditions and maintain one's identity in spite of the collective pressures of the environment made me stronger, more independent and better accepting of diversity.

Beloved family – left to right: Grandmother, Esther Feldman; mother, Eva Manevick; self and daughter, Alida Lechter, 1974

Frolicking in bubble bath, circa 1991

I have devoted most of my professional life to working in and for non-profit institutions, both educational and artistic. In Colombia, where I was born, I worked as a Humanities teacher and had the opportunity to open the eyes and minds of hundreds of high school students to the pleasures of Art, the joys of Literature and the challenges of Philosophy. As a teacher, there were always two or three students in every group who inspired me to be better. As a frequent traveler, there are occasionally a couple of tour companions who seem to be on the same wavelength. In both cases, it is like sharing a common past, although we may have totally different backgrounds. Most importantly, we establish a bond that takes us into the future.

Later I became the first female Executive Director for B'nai B'rith International, succeeding two rabbis, older and male, of course. Frequent travel to visit 21 volunteer groups in seven countries throughout Central America and the Caribbean taught me to pack light, be flexible, and, when staying at someone's home, smile for breakfast. Local interests and personal preferences influenced my work, but I was able to offer valuable training in areas such as time management, group dynamics, fund raising and communication skills.

Throughout it all, my love for art and the recognition of its power to transform lives has been a constant. During a difficult period of my life, I supported myself

162

as an art dealer, one who enjoyed explaining the different techniques involved in making a woodprint, an etching and a silk screen. After several years, I was pleased to be appointed to serve as a member of the Board of Directors of the Museum of Modern Art 'La Tertulia' in Cali.

Fast forward to life in Miami. After marrying a wonderful man who had been best man at my first wedding 30 years before, I quickly became involved in my new community and started to participate in the activities of the City of Miami Commission on the Status of Women. This involved editing and co-editing the quarterly newsletter, producing some TV programs on issues of particular interest to women (i.e., Body Image, Cosmetic Surgery and Self-Esteem, Caregivers Facing Death) and lobbying for increased funding for programs related to women.

In the past two years, I have parlayed my interest in the arts, my writing skills and my interest in the community by writing grants for organizations that have

My husband, George Safirstein, MD, and me in Paulet Island (home to thousands of Adelie Penguins), Antartica, 1999

special meaning for me. The Miami Beach Garden Conservancy offers 'Arts in the Garden', performances and exhibitions presented in a beautiful natural setting, while the Sister Cities Program provides opportunities to meet people from other countries, explore their heritage and learn from their culture.

To be adopted into the Goddesses Project has turned me inward. It has made me appreciate myself as I recognize my limitations. It has made me feel part of a collective female super-entity that goes beyond each one of us, but needs us as individuals to exist. For this opportunity, I am grateful.

Girl's school, Sana'a, Yemen
(photograph taken by school girl), 2000

Pola's Menu

- Tuna Antipasto
- Chickpea Salad
- Roasted Peppers
- Seafood Pasta
- Fresh Bread and Breadsticks
- Tiramisu

notes:

Dinner with Goddess Pola

An easy Italian Feast. Why Italian? Love the country! Had a very special relationship with a witty Italian artist… maybe. There is, however, something else: A photograph taken on July 30, 1967. I am holding my newborn son, Ilán, who is ten days old on his older brother's birthday, Adrián being three, years old. Everyone who has looked at that photograph asks who is the brunette, Italian-looking woman and that cute baby. Was there a past life as an Italian? Some people have found a slight resemblance with Sofia Loren. WOW!

But back to food and some basic influences. My mother was a very strong woman. Widowed after three years of marriage, she was left with two young daughters. We moved in with my grandparents and lived with them for almost seven years. In spite of the arrangements, or perhaps because of the freedom they offered her, she led a very independent life. She was the first woman to drive a car in Cali, Colombia and the only woman to play poker with men, in addition to her rummy games with her lady friends. She spent most of her life working for the community, including her own Jewish community and the community-at-large. I have inherited her independent ways, her commitment to others, her directness and her ability to make important decisions quickly.

My mother liked to cook and she loved to use her hands creatively. Whether crocheting the borders for baby diapers or dishtowels, or knitting sweaters or shawls (all her friends had at least one), she was never without a huge straw basket full of handicrafts by her side. Food preparation was to be simple, fast and enjoyable, and you were not to spend a lot of time in the kitchen. I agree. You need to be able to enjoy your company and not slave over a stove. What brings me joy is connecting with people. What a great feeling!

- Some day, I say to myself, I'll start exercising regularly and lose some weight.
- Some day, I say to myself, I'll write to my friends.
- Some day, I say to myself, I'll complete the novel that I started over a dozen years ago.
- Some day, I say to myself, I'll be closer to God.

notes:

Antipasto Platter

This platter includes recipes for a tuna antipasto and roasted peppers, which were my mother's recipes, as well as a chickpea salad and both green & black olives.

Tuna Antipasto

This dish is best made the day before and refrigerated overnight. It will last a long time and the flavor will actually improve with age.

Ingredients:
- 2 cans of water-packed tuna (white or regular, depending on your budget)
- 1 jar of Italian garden vegetable pickles
- 1/2 cup of catsup
- 1/4 cup of mustard
- hot sauce

Method:
- Drain the tuna.
- Dice the pickles into 1/2 inch pieces.
- Mix tuna, pickles and seasonings to taste. Stir.
- Keep refrigerated at least overnight.

Chickpea Salad

Ingredients:
- 1 can chickpeas (garbanzos)
- 4 scallions (green onions)
- parsley
- olive oil
- Balsamic vinegar
- fresh ground pepper

Method:
- Rinse and drain chickpeas.
- Chop scallions and parsley finely.
- Mix ingredients and season to taste.
- Refrigerate if not used immediately.

notes:

notes:

Roasted Peppers

This is another recipe that is best done the day before and left in the refrigerator overnight.

Ingredients:
- 3 peppers
  (green, red and yellow look great)
- olive oil
- vinegar
- 4 garlic cloves
- salt and pepper to taste

Method:
- Pre-heat oven to 250°–275°.
- Roast peppers moistened with olive oil in a low oven for 1 hour.
- Allow to cool and remove peel (peppers will be very soft).
- Smash garlic cloves with some salt.
- Cover peppers with mixture and season to taste.
- Place in a glass jar and marinate in olive oil and vinegar overnight.

Seafood Pasta

This recipe can be adapted for kosher use by omitting the shrimp.

Ingredients:
- 2 fish filets, diced in 1-inch cubes
- 12 medium-sized peeled shrimp (leave tail on)
- 1 onion chopped
- 1 green pepper, diced
- 1 tomato, diced
- 1 clove of garlic
- 2 tablespoons olive oil
- 2 cups very hot water
- oregano, thyme, salt and pepper
- your favorite cooked pasta

Method:
- Lightly brown onion and pepper in hot olive oil.
- Add tomato and cook until soft.
- Add fish, shrimp, water and seasonings. Stir carefully.
- Cook 3-5 minutes until shrimp turns pink and sauce has thickened.
- Serve over cooked pasta.

notes:

Tiramisu

This recipe is not the traditional tiramisu. It does not use eggs and it replaces traditional mascarpone (heavy fat content) with ricotta.

Ingredients:
- 1 1/2 cups ricotta cheese (may be low-fat)
- 1/2 cup sugar
- 1/4 cup cream
- 1 teaspoon vanilla
- 1/2 cup coffee liqueur (Tia Maria, Kahlua)
- 1/2 cup espresso (or strong coffee)
- 1 package ladyfingers
- cocoa powder

Method:
- Beat ricotta with sugar until well-blended.
- Stir in cream.
- Mix coffee liqueur with coffee in a deep dish.
- Dip ladyfingers in coffee mixture; place in a rectangular or square deep serving dish.
- Cover with 1/3 of the cheese mixture.
- Repeat the last two steps twice more, ending with cheese mixture.
- Sprinkle cocoa powder on top.
- Refrigerate until serving.

You don't get to choose how you are going to die. Or when. You can only decide how you're going to live. Now.

Joan Baez

Rozelle Putnam

Smyrna, GA

What the hell — you might be right, you might be wrong — but don't just avoid.

Katharine Hepburn

Rozelle Putnam

Okavango Delta in Botswana, 1996

Sydney Harbor, 1998

I was born in Cape Town, South Africa. Maybe it was a good time to be born at the end of the Great Depression, as I just haven't had time to be depressed ever again. My life has been so wonderfully full, I wouldn't change one single day. I have chosen to live this charmed life with an attitude of optimism and to capture the full expression of each moment in all that I say and do.

school and get out into the world on our own, seeing as much as possible of our incredible world. I did this. Still in my teens, I sailed to London. It took three weeks and this was no cruise ship, I might add. After working there for a year, I tried my luck in Germany, which was a real challenge. Next was Namibia on the west coast of Africa for ten years. I lived on the edge of the Namibian desert, famous for the man-eating welwitchia plant and the highest shifting sand dunes in the world. This is where my beautiful daughter Othene was born, so it will always hold a special place in my heart.

Holding up the pipeline in Alaska, 1991

Magical Island of Bali, 1997

I have a thirst for the beauty of different cultures and a hunger for far-away places. I am driven to experience the wonders of our amazing planet as I lace up my hiking boots and see for myself all that's waiting out there for me to explore. My joy is sharing all I have learned with intimate groups of like-minded friends as we trek through the rain forests of Sumatra or safari in wildest Africa. I am driven by a force of being in the 'here and now,' being fully present in today in this moment. I seize each opportunity and savor each person in my life.

From there I spent a few years in Angola, so we all had to switch from speaking German to Portuguese, and eating cod fish now instead of brats. My life then took a decided twist. I went back to Cape Town for a while, which I feel is the most beautiful place on earth. I started traveling to the most extraordinary spots imaginable such as Madagascar, the Congo, Towanda, Burundi, Swaziland, Lesotho, Mauritius and Reunion.

I settled in Atlanta in the late 70's and then my passion really took hold. I started telling friends how wonderful South Africa was, and the next thing I knew I had an intrepid bunch of safarians setting off with their 'fearless leader' for the bush. That was the start of many

South Africans are geographically isolated. Because of this we are encouraged by our families to finish

tours I dreamt up and escorted to Antarctica, Easter Island, Tahiti, Australia, New Zealand, India, Nepal, Patagonia, Alaska, Chile, Ecuador/Galapagos, Egypt, Bali, Thailand and Singapore, to name but a few. In fact, I have now been to over 100 countries and all seven continents. With all this travel, I really don't have any other pastimes other than researching future adventures. I must admit, though, I love reading world history and spending a great deal of time pouring over maps and charts.

One of my most enlightening moments was recently in central Thailand where a Buddhist monk blessed my little Emerald Buddha, which is from a chip off the original Emerald Buddha in a temple in Bangkok. I have had some remarkable experiences such as hot-air ballooning over the Serengeti, conducting the Hanover Symphony orchestra, flying over Mount Everest in a

'Mother' in the rain forest of Sumatra, 1997

small aircraft and climbing in the rain forest to see the Orangutans in Sumatra. (They touched my red hair thinking I was family.) I have gone elephant trekking

Bedouin tent in Wadi Rum, 1990

in northern Thailand, swum with penguins off the shores of Cape Town, searched for the three-toed sloth in the Amazon jungle and stayed in a Bedouin tent in the desert in Jordan.

I have experienced the world of high fashion and the beauty and joys of motherhood. My granddaughters Samantha and Grace were born in America, so this has been a magical time playing Granny. I am grateful for all of these passages, content with how the lessons have molded me and satisfied with who I am and how I got here. I am grateful to all the amazing and interesting people who have shared my journey, teaching me their cultures and customs. It is the freedom of my body, freedom of my expression and freedom of my heart that makes up my soul. I invite you into my world of playfulness, fun, laughter and optimism. Join me on an adventure to some far-away undiscovered land. To all whom I love, to all who have loved me, I say thank you for sharing in my journey. *Rozelle Putnam*

You can contact Rozelle by email: rozellep@aol.com

Rozelle's Menu

- Seafood Bisque
- Wine
- Cape Malay Bobotie
- Deviled Carrots
- Tipsy Trifle

notes:

Dinner with Goddess Rozelle

My hunt in Africa was a roaring success! I tracked down all the ingredients for my bobotie! Even though there are more recipes of this Cape Malay favorite than spots on a leopard, I would like to share my version with you. Having been born and bred in Cape Town, like most fellow South Africans, I have always had this love affair with the local cuisine.

In the late 1700's, the Cape of Good Hope was under Dutch rule. Many people were sent there from the Dutch East Indies (Indonesia) to work for the Dutch settlers. Rice was the staple food that had to be imported from Batavia. This boring little diet cried out for spices such as pepper, ginger, nutmeg, cloves, coriander, turmeric, cinnamon and saffron. So the monotonous diet was blended with these spices and Cape Malay Cuisine was born, with its characteristic flavors. Cape Malay dishes such as bobotie, sosaties, bredies, kebabs, samoosas, sambals and blatjang (chutney), of which there are many, have survived up to the present day.

"Geniet u kos"
(Enjoy this meal)

174

Seafood Bisque

Cape Aghulas, the southernmost tip of Africa, is the meeting point of the Atlantic and Indian Oceans. Consequently, South Africa boasts an abundance of wonderful seafood. I therefore feel a seafood soup would be a great way to start our meal. This recipe is quick and easy. The final result belies the simple ingredients and method. Serves 6.

Ingredients:
- 1 1/2 cups tomato pureé
- 1 can pea soup
- 1 1/2 cups milk
- 1 cup sherry
- 1 cup crab meat
- 1 cup peeled shrimp
- 1 cup diced lobster
- 1 teaspoon oregano
- dash of tabasco
- salt and pepper to taste
- 1/4 pint whipping cream, unwhipped

Method:
- Mix all ingredients except the whipping cream.
- Cook over a slow heat.
- Add the cream and simmer till warm.

notes:

Bobotie—A Cape Malay Favorite

Original Bobotie recipes call for minced leg of lamb, which would produce a coarser texture. I prefer to use ground beef, which is certainly a lot easier to deal with. This recipe should serve 8 (or a hungry 6). All the spices should be readily available in North America, though I was fortunate to be able to collect them from the source.

Ingredients:
- 2 thick slices of white bread (remove crusts)
- 1 1/2 cups milk
- 2 pounds ground beef (or lamb)
- 1 tablespoon smooth apricot jam
- 2 large finely chopped onions
- 2 tablespoons fruit chutney
- 1 extra large beaten egg
- 1/4 cup slivered almonds
- 5 teaspoons butter or two tablespoons vegetable oil
- 2 tablespoons lemon juice
- 2 finely grated rinds of lemons
- 5 tablespoons cream (optional)
- 5 bay leaves (or 8 fresh lemon leaves)
- 4 to 5 tablespoons curry powder (depending on how spicy you like it but do not use too much)
- 3 freshly crushed cloves of garlic
- 2 teaspoons ground ginger (or 1 inch fresh ginger root peeled and finely chopped)
- 2 teaspoons ground cumin
- 2 teaspoons ground coriander (3 cloves)
- salt and freshly ground black pepper to taste

Topping Ingredients:
- 3 extra large eggs, beaten
- 1 1/2 cups milk
- 2 pinches of turmeric
- salt and pepper to taste

Method:
- Pre-heat oven to 350°.
- Soak bread in milk for about 10 minutes, then mash. Put aside.
- Fry the onions in oil until translucent.
- Sprinkle in curry mixture, add meat and cook till done.
- Stir in cumin, coriander, cloves, ginger, garlic and apricot jam.
- Place in ovenproof dish and spoon the soaked mashed bread into mixture.
- Pour the beaten eggs, cream, lemon juice, lemon rind, and almonds into the mixture and mix thoroughly, but lightly.
- Roll bay leaves into spikes and press into mixture.
- Bake for 15 minutes.
- While this is cooking, prepare the topping by eating the eggs and stirring in the milk. Add turmeric, salt and pepper to taste.
- Remove the 'almost' bobotie from the oven.
- Pour over the egg mixture topping and bake for another 30 minutes, until egg mixture sets.

176

Deviled Carrots

Ingredients:
- 1/4 pound butter
- 12 to18 baby carrots, halved
- 3 tablespoons coarse brown sugar
- 1 1/2 teaspoons mustard
- 4–5 drops Tabasco
- 1/2 teaspoon salt

Method:
- Melt butter.
- Sauté carrots till reasonably soft (about 6 minutes).
- Add rest of ingredients and simmer for 10 minutes.

notes:

Tipsy Trifle

For most of us, British cooking is rather blah with one exception…the 'Trifle'. This came to South Africa during Queen Victoria's reign and has been one of the most popular creative desserts right into the 21st century. I feel the success lies in one's decorating skills, and so the trifle should be presented in colorful layers in a large, attractive stemmed-glass bowl. This should serve 6 adequately.

Ingredients:
- 1 large sponge cake
- 1/2 cup strawberry jam, slightly melted
- 4 large teaspoons brown sherry
- 1 pint custard
- 1 packet each red and green Jell-O
- 10 small broken meringues, optional

Topping Ingredients:
- 1 cup whipped cream, in soft peaks
- 1 ounce pecans or almond flakes, slightly roasted
- 20 maraschino cherries, with stalks
- 2 sticks of angelica, cut to look like leaves

Method:
- Prepare the red and green Jell-O and allow to set.
- Cut the cake into squares and spread jam, sandwich style.
- Place a layer of cake in bowl, and sprinkle with sherry.
- Spoon on some warm custard, allowing it to run.
- Add pieces of meringue, then red Jell-O, a layer of cake and a layer of green Jell-O. Then keep layering with cake, sherry, meringue, jello and custard till the bowl is full.
- Cover with cling wrap and refrigerate.
- Just before serving, spread the cream evenly.
- Decorate with nuts, cherries and angelica.

When we can begin to take our failures non-seriously,

it means we are ceasing to be afraid of them.

It is of immense importance to learn to laugh at ourselves.

Katherine Mansfield

Sally Vickers

Malibu, CA

We don't see things as they are,
we see things as we are.

Anaïs Nin

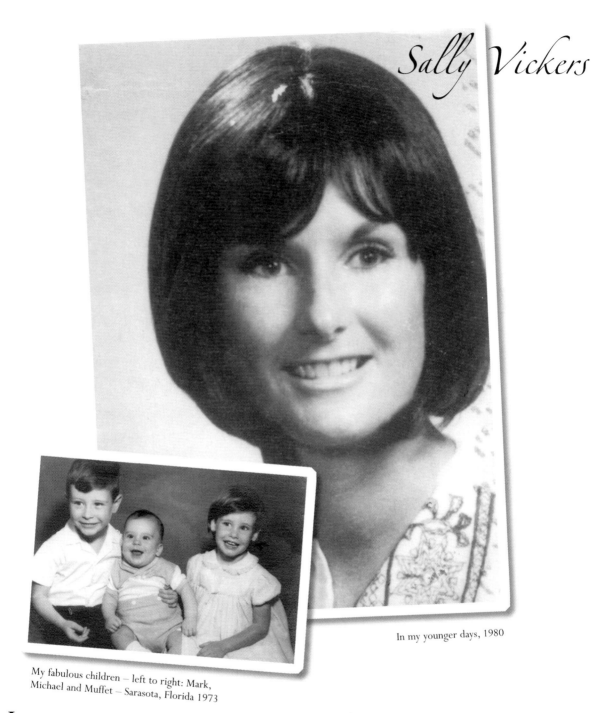

Sally Vickers

In my younger days, 1980

My fabulous children — left to right: Mark, Michael and Muffet — Sarasota, Florida 1973

I was born on April Fool's Day. I was morphed onto the planet feeling totally unprepared. I was seeing clairvoyantly and experiencing a 'knowing' on many different levels. Revelations, Catholicism and my father 'the Pope' leading us in the family rosary every night are all vivid memories. At five, I was lifted seven feet off the ground by an eagle in our backyard in New York. I remember being lifted by my coat collar and hanging in mid-air. My father ran to me, threw his pipe at the eagle and I landed on my head. I was disappointed that I couldn't fly with that eagle.

Island girl, Tahiti, 1994

With my dear cat, Fluffbutt, now passed away – Malibu, CA 1986

My next psychic memory was shopping with my mother at Sak's Fifth Avenue. I was eight, wandering around the store, when an announcement came over the loudspeaker—"Attention all Sak's shoppers, we are offering a special sale of unusual gifts, all one of a kind." I hurried over, leaving mom behind in the dressing room, and saw the most unusual little lady. She had a price tag on her toe, a smile on her face and sparkling love in her eyes. I took her hand and eagerly looked around for a way to pay for her, since I had only 10 cents in my pocket. The unusual lady said to me, "I'm free to the right girl. I won't let you fall on your head and you'll never have to do homework." "Done deal," I said. This is how I got my guide that I call 'little Annie Fanny with a heart of gold.' Only problem was, no one else could see her, which I thought was rather cool. We both agreed to keep this life simple.

The 'being dropped by an eagle' event was a further link to my psychic experiences. "Where am I?" I asked upon regaining consciousness. A rather loud voice echoed in my ear: "On a fool's errand again," and then I heard giggling. A rather attractive woman held me in front of a mirror and said how funny I was with my big ears. Trouble was, I couldn't see my reflection. Since I had no way of understanding, I decided it might be better to go through life with my eyes closed and my smile intact. I found words far more interesting than bodies… still do. I remember feeling how sweet this lifetime was going to be with this unusual gift I was given.

My school days were not always simple, though. I excelled in writing, while desperately struggling with math. I had my ESP tested by Australian scientists at Duke University. I didn't know if this was a lotto win or an imprisonment. I kept asking, "Who am I? And why am I here?" So Annie, one of my chosen guides in this lifetime, revealed much of the story to me. She shared that because of my unique psychic abilities, much of my knowledge would come from Spirit. I call this special knowing 'soul knowledge.' I love that I've got it. I have moved through life at an incredible speed, most importantly learning humor and compassion from my special guides in spirit. Through all the years of doing my work, the knowledge I've been shown has enriched my life beyond measure. "More," I keep saying, "I want to know everything."

Ger and me with our catch in Alaska, 1989

I lived in Sarasota, Florida, home of my tribal family. Becoming a mom of three by 22 was a circus event. It appears that three Gemini's had me lined up for this lifetime. I hung in there and didn't run away. My children have been great teachers and I've learned a lot. Sarasota is still home for my eldest son, Mark and his fiancée, the bright and beautiful Jennifer. My middle child, daughter Muffet, also resides in Sarasota. My youngest son, Michael (called the golden child by his siblings since he calls home once a week), lives with his dynamic and witty wife Kristin in Morristown, New Jersey.

What an exciting life this has been. I was the first woman in the state of Florida to be approved to take the 200-hour course in law enforcement, and passed. I moved from police work to using my psychic intuitive gifts, helping law enforcement in many states locate missing people and animals, as well as tracking down perps. In 1984, I assisted the family of a kidnapped man in South America. The man was being held for ransom. I was able to assure the family he was still alive and would be returned home safely. Other psychics said he was dead. He returned home after three months, thinner yet grateful to still be alive and with his family.

As adults, each of my children are committed to community service. Mark has his own construction company and, with his dog Simon, is part of the Sarasota Search & Rescue Team that locates and rescues missing persons. Muffet began Camp Florida Fishtails for handicapped children four years ago, with her recently departed husband Brian. They received the city of Sarasota's 'Hero of the Year' award in 2000 for their hard work in fundraising. She is presently negotiating with Sarasota County to donate land so she can run a full-time camp for the children to enjoy. Michael is General Manager for a company in Chatham, New Jersey, while also serving his community. He prefers to remain anonymous about his service work, although it has been noted and appreciated by many.

My kids and their loves — left to right: Mark, Jennifer, Muffet, Mike, Kris — NYC 2001

For the past 14 years I have lived in Malibu, California, with my partner in fun, Ger, a recently retired (and loving every minute of it) doctor. He grows orchids, enjoys gardening, and works out daily at Pepperdine University. Ger is an active saltwater fisherman with his personal best being a 304-pound tuna. I also love deep sea, stand-up fishing for the big tuna and wahoo, off the coast of Mexico. My personal best to date has been a 178-pound yellow fin tuna. Salmon fishing in Alaska is the best. Ger's biggest challenge is teaching me how to tie knots for fishing the big ones. Since I have dyslexia, I always reverse things. I teach him patience.

My current dreams include working with the Feds on profiling and locating criminals. I am also actively trying to publish my books *Exquisite Souls I & II*, as well as my children's book, *Santa's Last Christmas*.

Sally Vickers

You can contact Sally at:
www.pointmall.com/sally
You can contact Camp Fish Tales at:
www.campfishtales.com

Dinner *with* Goddess Sally

Here are some thoughts that come to mind when I begin to plan a meal. First I'd select music to cook by …opera, classical, jazz or golden oldies would be my choices. Whatever your choice, have the music match your mood. Use your 'sixth sense' when cooking, eliminating the need to always measure amounts. Experiment. Become a kitchen 'chanteuse'.

A lovely table for dining is a work of art. As a child, my job was to set the table. I loved Sundays best, because on that special day I could use the 'good' china, lace tablecloth and fine silverware. I decided early on that when I grew up, I would make every dinner a special dinner using the best I had. When my children were born, I began setting the dinner table using a variety of colors to suit the moods. Now, I always have my dining table set for two. It is easy to add more settings for guests. I set the table every evening for the next day. I use color, candles, fine crystal, linens and elegant plates to set the mood for my next dining experience. I feel we should garnish our tables as we would our souls, making the setting and the food appetizing.

So you've completed your meal (my offering is a dinner for four) and have just served it to your guests. Take a look at your masterpiece. Savor the beauty you have created, the colors, the textures and the table design. Savor the moment with your family members, or guests, before everyone digs in to this nutritious abundant offering and the food disappears in a wink.

Divine wine is an all-time favorite with dinner. Choose your wines as carefully as you would choose your soul mates. Offer both red and white. Sparkling non-alcoholic wines are also available. I like to serve cool spring water in large crystal goblets, too.

Most importantly, bless all that you have. Enjoy!

Sally's Menu

- Smoked Fish, Celery Sticks and Fresh Organic Veggies
- Wine
- Heavenly Halibut
- Popeye's Creamed Spinach
- Sliced Peppers Yellow, Orange, and Red
- Low-Fat Jell-O Dessert with Fruit or
- Yogurt Cream Cheese Pie

notes:

Appetizers

Since we eat healthy and light, I usually serve smoked fish, or celery sticks and red peppers garnished with a seasoning called 'Spike.' Fresh organic veggies right out of our garden make a pretty picture.

Heavenly Halibut

I prefer to catch my own in California or, better yet, Alaska. Fresh is best, yet frozen is acceptable. Halibut is flash frozen in Alaska and holds well in the freezer up to 6 months. The cooked halibut is a crusty brown color with the spinach adding the color green. I like to think colors, breathe colors and eat colors. I often add sliced red, orange and yellow bell peppers as a garnish to enhance the dinner dance. You will love serving this yummy, delicate halibut. What a treat!

Ingredients:
- 4 halibut filets
- 1 cup whole or 2% milk for a marinade
- 3 cups Betty Crocker Potato Spuds
- 2 to 3 tablespoons 'Spike' seasoning, the original all-purpose version
- 2 teaspoons of Chef Paul's Magic Seasoning for seafood.
- 1 tablespoon of Parmesan cheese, adding more to your taste
- salt and pepper to taste
- 1 tablespoon capers
- 2 tablespoons pine nuts
- 1 lemon, thinly sliced
- 4 sprigs of fresh basil
- 1 plastic storage bag with a strong seal. I use the larger freezer bags.
- Canola oil for basting fish

notes:

Method:
- Take fresh (or defrosted) halibut and trim off any dark pieces. Cut into serving portions.
- Place halibut in a flat container and cover with milk. Cover and refrigerate about 2–4 hours. The longer the better. Overnight is okay, too.
- Preheat oven to 450°.
- In large plastic bag, mix the Betty Crocker potato spuds, Spike, Chef Paul's Magic Seasoning, Parmesan cheese, salt and pepper. Seal the bag and shake well.
- Drain capers and set aside.
- Lightly brown pine nuts. Drain, then set aside.
- Remove fish from milk, drain and blot with paper towels. Set aside.
- Lightly brush canola oil on fish, both sides. Using tongs, place fish pieces one at a time in the bag and coat both sides well. Place coated fish in baking dish.
- Sprinkle fish with Parmesan cheese, then add pine nuts and capers.
- Bake 12 minutes in hot oven. Cooking time depends on the thickness of fish. Test the doneness at intervals. Do not over cook. Fish should be flaky inside.
- Place under broiler for a minute or so to brown topping.
- Remove from oven, and serve on your very best dishes. Garnish with a sprig of fresh basil and a lemon slice.

Popeye's Creamed Spinach

This spinach has an attitude. Even your kids will like it. Are you ready to ascend into a higher state of consciousness? Watch the smiles on the faces of all you serve.

Ingredients:
- 4 1/2 pounds fresh spinach, stems removed
- 1 pint half and half
- 1/4 cup chopped shallots
- 1/2 stick unsalted butter, cut into 4 pieces
- 1/3 cup grated Parmesan cheese
- 1 teaspoon spicy mustard
- 1/2 teaspoon salt
- 1/8 teaspoon cayenne pepper

Method:
- Lightly steam spinach. Drain and chop. This can be done the day before.
- In a large saucepan, add half and half and shallots. Over medium high heat, bring to a boil. Adjust the heat and boil for another 15 minutes until mixture is reduced to a cup.
- Reduce heat to medium and stir butter into your half and half mixture until melted.
- Add Parmesan cheese, mustard, salt and cayenne pepper.
- Add spinach, cook for about 6-8 minutes, stirring frequently.
- Serve to your guests.

Low-Cal, Sugar-Free Jell-O

This is so quick and easy. I call this 'Cerebral Musings.'

Ingredients:
- 2 (6) ounce pkgs. of sugar-free Jell-O in 2 different flavors. I like Wild Strawberry and Mandarin Orange.
- 1 cup chopped nuts of your choice
- 2 bananas, sliced
- 2 cups low-cal Cool Whip
- chocolate sprinkles

Method:
- Mix both packages of Jell-O together in a large bowl, directions are on the box
- Let Jell-O sit in refrigerator for 30 minutes, until slightly jelled.
- Add chopped nuts
- Add sliced bananas, or any other fruit of your choice.
- Add 2 cups of Cool Whip and blend with Jell-O and fruit.
- Chill in refrigerator for 1 hour.
- Garnish with Cool Whip and chocolate sprinkles.

Yogurt Cream Cheese Pie

I call this 'Blame it on the Devil.' You can buy prepared graham cracker crust.

Crust Ingredients:
- 2 cups crushed graham crackers
- 1/2 cup butter
- Pam cooking spray
- 2 tablespoons honey
- 1 teaspoon cinnamon

Method:
- Melt butter with honey.
- Mix cinnamon with graham crackers.
- Add dry mixture to butter and honey mixture, blending well.
- Press into a 9 inch glass pie plate.

Filling Ingredients:
- 8 ounces softened cream cheese
- 1 1/2 cup yogurt
- 1 1/2 cup honey
- 1 teaspoon vanilla
- 1 rind of 1/2 lemon

Method:
- Beat together all ingredients.
- Pour into piecrust and refrigerate for 3 hours.

Avoiding danger is no safer in the long run than outright exposure. The fearful are caught as often as the bold.

Helen Keller

Sandra Storrar

Roswell, GA

I am going to love myself and live my life authentically, intuitively attuned to my heart and soul.

Paula M. Reeves

Sandra Storrar

High school senior prom with ski partner – Florida, 1960

Just 5 years old, 1947

The challenge of writing a biography for this cookbook has been interesting. I can easily write recipes, yet when faced with the task of writing about myself, an entirely different energy appears. I have wrestled with this energy, as I have been trained to focus on my creations, not myself. I finally realized that I am a creation also. So, to begin....

One way to approach my life is from the facts, and I want to share them, honoring what has been. I spent my early years in a small mill town in northwestern Pennsylvania, rich with immigrant cultures. My life was no exception, being second-generation American with

The day I earned my PhD, 1980

University President's Inaugural Ball, 1993

four grandparents who had emigrated from Scotland and England. As a child, I remember the many different languages I heard and the many wonderful types of food that were always around. It was not unusual to have Polish desserts at an Italian dinner at Christmas, along with English tea. My father had a catering service, thus food was a part of my life from the beginning. I often helped in the kitchen, so I could spend time with him.

In my early teens, my family moved to Florida after purchasing a small family-type restaurant. I was expected to work there after school and on weekends, either cooking or assisting in the dining room. One of my challenges has been to modify my thinking to cooking for only four to six, as I learned to cook for hundreds. I always prepare too much food and my guests have to endure the "Let me give you some to take home," routine.

I left home at age 17, only returning for brief visits once gone. It never occurred to me to live at home again; there was a world out there to see and experience. Over the years, I earned three college degrees, with the highest being a doctorate in Political Science. Much of my life in my twenties and thirties was about working a full-time management position at a large urban university while attending night classes to earn my advanced degrees. After I earned my doctorate, my life moved in a direction that was totally a surprise, a direction that has brought me great joy. Consciously, I began my spiritual journey. This journey has had incredible twists and turns, an unending process.

I spent many years in management positions at this urban university, the highest being that of Assistant Vice President. Managing a large staff offered me opportunities to integrate my spiritual principles with my management style. I created an environment of learning for my management team that surpassed all of our expectations. My next experience was in a fast-paced, high technology industry where I spent three and a half years. This new work experience threw me into a company that never stopped changing. I traveled the majority of my time, building a significant stash of frequent flyer miles on most major airlines. My pace of learning increased ten-fold during this experience, and staying consistent with my values and beliefs was a constant challenge.

In addition to working with management teams, my satisfaction has been in creating a home environment and in cooking to entertain family and friends. I enjoy the process of creating a warm and comfortable home. I like people to come in and to enjoy, be 'at home' and 'at peace.' Since my siblings and I grew up in a kitchen, when we have family gatherings for holidays, we are all in the kitchen cooking meals together. I purchased the home I currently own because it has a large, comfortable kitchen that allows a group to cook together. This love is being transmitted to the new generation in our family as my daughter, niece and nephew also join in the fun.

My desire for community is ever present. This past Christmas, with the assistance of several special friends, I prepared a buffet dinner for more than fifty friends.

On snowshoes in SunVally, 1993

As I looked around during the evening, hearing the conversations, seeing the candlelight, enjoying the trays of food and warm fire, delighting in the smells of the season, I felt true happiness and joy. The same is true when I do a small dinner party. I look around at the faces of my guests aglow in the candlelight, marveling at how special it is to share good food and good conversation.

With my daughter, Jennifer, 2000

I love browsing antique shops and flea markets, finding treasures that can be recycled, bringing a new life to something old and wonderful. Another pleasure of mine is dancing of any kind. I love movement. I often use dance as a metaphor when I approach a situation. My life dance has been one of constant change and growth, always learning new steps. I move from ballet to salsa to tango. I am not always sure of the steps, although I do always hear the music. The lines from T.S. Elliott where he states that there is only 'the dance,' has been my mantra. I intend to keep dancing for a very long time.

At this time in my life, I feel such richness and depth. Integrity, bone honesty and being true to what really matters to me guides my life. I am now involved with the Center for Authentic Leadership as a part of their Future Thinking Group. My focus is to be a part of this learning community and move forward with my life toward a coaching/mentoring role. Coaching/mentoring is an experience where I can more consistently live my spiritual principles, using my gifts and competencies to make a difference. I am constantly in awe and amazement of what life offers me, if I stay conscious.

Dinner with Goddess Sandra

The sharing of an intimate meal with friends is at the top of my list of joyful experiences. Through the sharing of food, we have the opportunity to share who we are with those we love, nurturing each other in our journey through life. It is through the sharing of recipes that family and friends often transmit their culture and their love for each other. For many years, I have felt connected to friends with whom I've shared recipes. I love using a recipe given to me in that person's handwriting, feeling a connection as I cook their food. This is especially poignant if it is from a friend who is no longer living. I feel their life continues through my preparing their recipe.

Most often my dinner parties are for four to six people to keep the conversation intimate. I enjoy bringing an eclectic group of people together, creating opportunities for interesting conversation. I view creating a beautiful table as the 'set' for the evening. My table is done ahead of time, before the guests arrive. I like to do it alone, quietly creating. I use flowers and low candles (such as votives) to help create the mood. I enjoy being playful with holidays, like scattering shamrocks around the table in mid-March, using green candles too. To further set the mood for the evening, I place candles, in the kitchen and living room, keeping the tone of the evening consistent.

I am organized, preferring to have as much of the meal prepared ahead of time, so I can truly be with my guests. My kitchen is large with comfortable seating. Since everyone always converges on a kitchen, I usually serve appetizers on the island in the middle. I serve easy appetizers such as reduced-fat Jarlsberg cheese, goat Gouda and hommus. This is accompanied by crisp sliced apples, such as Pink Lady or Granny Smith with walnuts and a low-fat whole-wheat crackers. I serve a chilled Sauvignon Blanc, the same wine I use for the meal.

Sandra's Menu

- Cheese and Hummus
- Crackers and Sliced Apples
- Wine
- Strawberries and Feta Salad
- Sautéed Salmon Steaks
- Baked Rice
- Roasted Asparagus with Lemon
- Lemon Meringue Pie
- Coffee and Tea

notes:

Strawberries & Feta Salad

I found this recipe in a magazine and in using it discovered it tastes great with any vinaigrette dressing, even bottled. If I do not have orange juice on hand, I substitute bottled vinaigrette. I like the salad to be ready, including the dressing, which only requires combining the salad mixture with the dressing before serving.

Ingredients:
- 2 tablespoon orange juice
- 1 tablespoon white wine vinegar
- 2 teaspoon extra-virgin olive oil
- 3/4 teaspoon sugar
- 6 cups gourmet salad greens
- 1 cup quartered strawberries
- 1/4 cup (1 ounce) crumbled feta cheese

Method:
- Combine first four ingredients in a small bowl, stir with a whisk.
- Combine greens, strawberries and feta in a large bowl.
- Add salad dressing mixture to greens, tossing to coat.
- Serve immediately. Serves 6.

notes:

notes:

Sautéed Salmon Steaks

I often use tamari instead of using soy sauce as it is lower in sodium and tastes just the same.

Ingredients:
- 3 tablespoons butter or margarine, melted
- 3 teaspoons soy sauce, or tamari
- dash garlic powder
- 3 tablespoons olive oil
- 6 salmon steaks, 6 to 8 ounces each
- 12 lemon slices

Method:
- Combine butter, soy sauce and garlic powder.
- Heat oil in medium to large skillet.
- Add salmon steaks and baste with butter/soy sauce mixture. Cook about five minutes or until browned on one side.
- Turn, baste, place lemon slices on steaks.
- Cook until salmon flakes when tested with a fork. 6 servings.

Baked Rice and Roasted Asparagus with Lemon

I chose both a starch and a vegetable that can be cooked in the oven to facilitate the cooking process. Have both already in the oven, before guests arrive. Since the roasted asparagus calls for a higher temperature, I put it in the 350° oven for 30 minutes along with the rice. Sometimes the rice takes a little more time than the recipe indicates, depending on your oven.

Baked Rice Ingredients:
- 1/4 cup (1/2 stick) butter
- 1/4 cup chopped green onion (approximately 4 onions)
- 2 cups chicken broth (use low fat and low sodium)
- 1 cup brown rice
- 1 cup golden raisins
- 1/4 cup minced, fresh parsley
- 1/2 cup sunflower seeds

Baked Rice Method:
- Pre-heat oven to 350°.
- Melt butter in medium skillet over medium heat.
- Add onion and sauté until slightly softened. Transfer to 2-quart baking dish.
- Stir in remaining ingredients except sunflower seeds.
- Cover tightly and bake until broth has been absorbed, for about 45 minutes to an hour.
- Remove from oven. Using fork, mix in sunflower seeds and serve immediately. Serves 6 to 8.

Roasted Asparagus

Ingredients:
- 3 tablespoons fresh lemon juice
- 1 tablespoon extra-virgin olive oil
- 1 teaspoon finely grated lemon peel
- 36 asparagus spears, trimmed

Roasted Asparagus Method:
- Pre-heat oven to 450°.
- Mix lemon juice, oil and lemon peel in 15"x10"x2" glass baking dish.
- Add asparagus, turn to coat and sprinkle with salt and pepper.
- Roast asparagus until crisp-tender, turning occasionally, for about 20 minutes.
- Serve warm or at room temperature. 6 servings.

notes:

Single Pie Crust

This is a variation on a recipe I found years ago in a vegetarian cookbook. I modified it to use spelt flour, as I try to avoid wheat products. Spelt flour is more difficult to work with, yet tastes lighter than regular flour. If you are willing to be patient with this, it is a great pie crust. I ruffle the edges with my fingers, covering with foil for the first five to seven minutes of baking so as not to get too dark. Make your pie earlier in the day, giving you more time to enjoy your guests.

Ingredients:
- 1 cup spelt flour
- 1/3 cup cold butter
- 5–7 tablespoons low-fat buttermilk

Method:
- Pre-heat oven to 450°.
- Cut together flour and the cold butter. Use a pastry cutter or two forks. (If you use unsalted butter, add 1/4 teaspoon salt.)
- When the mixture is uniformly blended, add enough buttermilk so that the mixture holds together enough to form a ball.
- Cover the dough tightly and chill at least an hour.
- After one hour, roll out dough and place in pie pan. (I always use glass or ceramic pie pans as they look nicer.)
- Bake about 10 to 12 minutes.

notes:

Lemon Meringue Pie Filling

One of my favorite pie fillings was a recipe my father had for lemon meringue. Unfortunately, his recipe was not saved in its original form. This recipe is from the original *Joy of Cooking* cookbook, with a few modifications that I remember from my youth.

Ingredients:
- 1 1/2 cups sugar
- 6 tablespoons cornstarch
- 1/4 teaspoon salt
- 1/2 cup cold water
- 1/2 cup fresh lemon juice (about 6 lemons)
- 3 well-beaten egg yolks
- 2 tablespoons butter
- 1 1/2 cups boiling water
- 1 teaspoon grated lemon peel

Method:
- Stir sugar, cornstarch and salt into a 2 or 3 quart saucepan over medium heat, gradually blending in cold water and lemon juice.
- When mixture is smooth, add egg yolks and butter, blending thoroughly.
- Stir constantly, slowly adding boiling water. Bring the mixture to a full boil, stirring gently.
- As it begins to thicken, reduce the heat, simmering slowly for 1 minute.
- Remove from heat and stir in grated lemon peel.
- Pour into baked pie shell.
- You're now ready to add the meringue topping before baking.

notes:

Meringue Topping

Ingredients:
- egg whites
- 1/4 teaspoon cream of tartar
- 3–4 tablespoons sugar
- 1/2 teaspoon vanilla

Method:
- Pre-heat oven to 450°.
- Whip egg whites until frothy.
- Add cream of tartar. Continue whipping until whites are stiff, but not dry, until they stand in peaks that lean over slightly when the beater is removed.
- Beat in sugar, one tablespoon at a time. Whip until desired sweetness is achieved. Do not over beat.
- Beat in vanilla.
- Spread over filled pie and bake 10 to 15 minutes, or until meringue is slightly golden brown on top.
- Cool before serving.

What's terrible is to pretend that the second-rate is first-rate.

To pretend that you don't need love when you do;

or you like your work when you know quite well

you're capable of better.

Doris Lessing

Sharon O'Connor

Dunwoody, GA

*Mistakes are part of the
dues one pays for a full life.*

Sophia Loren

Sharon O'Connor

High school and the beginning of the goddess, 1972

I was born near Pittsburgh, Pennsylvania. Growing up, I went to Catholic School. I had a less than desirable childhood. It was very fragmented and unstable due to alcoholism and many other dysfunctional problems with the grown-ups in my family.

I married at 19 and started a family, giving birth to my daughter Jackie. It was during this same period that I went to real estate school, so I could help support the family. My working in real estate enabled us to purchase a duplex at a very low cost, having the mortgage covered by the rent we received from the other half of our property. It was my first major success as a young adult and it felt good.

Bathing beauty, Aruba, 1992

When one is having kids, raising a family, keeping a home and working part-time, years pass in a blur of activities. Somewhere along the way, I got a divorce. Also, by this time, I had my son James and my second daughter Jordi. Raising a family as a single parent is definitely a way to test one's perseverance and faith.

Ma Familia — Front row — daughter Jordi; left to right: daughter, Jackie, me and son James, north Georgia mountains, 1990

I moved to Atlanta in 1986 to start a new life. As a full-time working single mother of three children, I have been quite busy over the years. I have good kids and feel they are my greatest accomplishment. I am fortunate to be their mom.

President's Award Trip, Hawaii, 1996
Left to right: Jackie, me, Jordi

I always knew I was a healer, but didn't know how to use this skill. I went to massage school for six months in 1990. Besides learning massage, I studied healing herbs and other holistic healing methods. I was taught the essence of how to use my desire to heal the sick. This profound work also healed me, as I traveled along my path of self-discovery. I became a Silva graduate. In a basic Silva weekend course, I learned how to heal people at a distance with prayer and visualization. Amazing as it may be, it works.

I realized I needed to go more mainstream and enrolled in school to secure an RN degree. In 1996, I graduated nursing school, the year the Olympics came to Georgia. It was an Olympic year for me personally, starting yet another cycle of life. I now had an even more expanded way to engage people in healing. I've worked in many areas of nursing, from operating rooms to the nursery. Each hospital has its unique opportunities for healing. All the jobs I've had since getting my degree have been in some field of healing. Whether in nursing or medical sales or hospice consulting, the field of healing has given me a chance to serve society in a very positive way.

There have been disappointments along the way, for sure. Yet, committing to spiritual growth has kept me grounded through these times. What is that old saying, "I never promised you a rose garden?" I identify with this. Even though all is not perfect, joy still fills my life. I am happy and attempting to flow through life in the spirit of expectancy. And, I still feel glamorous.

Being a goddess at home, Atlanta, 1997

At the Capri Palace Hotel, Capri, Italy
with my sister goddess Kathy, 2001

I have created a wonderful family of friends here in Georgia. I am especially grateful to my best friend, Kathy, for all her love and support throughout the years. I also want to thank Hollis and Pamela for their loving support. Pamela is my spirit sister. Most of all I would like to thank God for all the blessings and love I feel from Spirit. This is truly living for me. 'Just a closer walk with Thee' is my quest for the future. My underlying motivation on the planet is my desire to see people get well. When every layer is stripped away, this is my core truth. Even if it's just a kind word or gesture, it can heal. This is my reason for being.

Sharon O'Connor

Sharon's Menu

- Olive Pâté
- Wine
- Gorgonzola Penne Pasta
- Succulent & Spicy Fish Stew
- Crème Brulé
- Coffee

notes:

Dinner with Goddess Sharon

I like to think of myself as an Italian Goddess. I am in love with Italy and all things that represent that country. The menu I have selected is easy, yet impressive. I know this menu will delight your guests.

And, of course, let's not forget wine. I always give the choice of red or white, estimating about two glasses per person.

Olive Pâté Appetizer

Ingredients:
- 1 large can of black olives (pitted)
- juice of 1/2 lemon
- 2 ounces butter
- 4 teaspoons extra virgin olive oil
- 6 tablespoons Italian bread crumbs
- sea salt and cracked pepper to taste
- 1 tomato, chopped
- 1 sprig of Italian parsley
- 1 loaf of bread, with great crust

Method:
- Mix first 6 ingredients in a food processor, or mixer.
- Place pâté in a favorite serving dish, top with chopped tomatoes, and garnish with a sprig of parsley.
- Serve with warm crusty bread. Yum.

notes:

Gorgonzola Penne Pasta

This is the *prima course*, or first course. It is easy and impressive, a great basic dish. I like to garnish with walnuts, adding a tasty crunch. It also tastes great as a main dish by adding chicken or ham.

Ingredients:
- 1/2 cup gorgonzola blue cheese
- 1/2 cup pecorino romano cheese, look in deli section of your grocery
- 1/2 cup whipping cream
- 1 pkg. penne pasta

Method:
- Cook penne pasta according to directions. Don't over cook your pasta. It tastes great when firm.
- Mix all other ingredients in your pan and cook over low heat until mixture thickens.
- Combine and serve.

Here are five pasta-cooking tips that I use:

(1) Use a large soup pot and fill it half full with hot water.

(2) Add 2 tablespoons salt and bring to a rapid boil.

(3) Add pasta and stir every minute or so to prevent sticking.

(4) Drain pasta when it is still firm, or *al dente*. Don't rinse.

(5) Enjoy, Enjoy, Enjoy. Life is short.

Succulent & Spicy Fish Stew

This second course is a signature dish of a famous Italian restaurant here in Atlanta. I visited this restaurant five times before finally convincing the chef to share his secrets. Preparing this dish the first time took two days. To shorten the time, I devised a way to make it fast and easy. This is my family's favorite. Watch your guests' expressions, as they taste this succulent dish. This can also be served over pasta to create a one-pot dish.

RAO sauce is out of New York and is available at Bed, Bath and Beyond. The Arrabbiata sauces can be found in most Publix and Kroger food stores in the south. These two sauces add ZEST, because they have a little hot spice from hot peppers. I use mostly the light green and red chile peppers when making this from scratch. When you buy the sauce in a jar, all you need to do is heat it up. Serve with warm garlic toast.

Ingredients:
- 1 large jar of RAO's or Arrabbiata sauce
- 1 can of chicken broth
- 1/4 cup chopped parsley
- 1/2 cup dry white wine
- 1 3/4 pounds fresh mussels (check expiration date and clean them according to package)
- 1/2 pound white fish (cod or orange roughy)
- 1/2 pound shrimp
- sea salt and cracked pepper to taste

Method:
- Combine sauce, chicken broth and wine in large pot. Heat till almost boiling.
- Add the white fish and cook for 4-5 minutes.
- Add shrimp and mussels.
- Simmer for another 7 minutes and you're done.

notes:

Easy Crème Brulé

When Napoleon conquered Italy and stole treasures to take back to France, I think he took Crème Brulé. Oh, and let's not forget that the Mona Lisa hangs in the Louvre in Paris. The French say Napoleon bought it. The Italians say Napoleon stole it. Oh my. Well anyway, this dessert is simple and yet so grand. It truly reminds me of Mona. Get ready for oohs and aahs. This is a decadent finale to a sumptuous Italian feast

You will need 2 large pie pans
(glass or Corning)

Ingredients:
- 2 cups fresh raspberries
- 10 egg yolks
  Strain them to ensure no white is left.
  This is the secret to this recipe.
- 13 tablespoons of sugar
- 4 cups heavy whipping cream
- 2 tablespoons of vanilla
  I like a lot of vanilla.
- raw sugar to sprinkle on as a topping

Method:
- Divide raspberries in the 2 pie pans, covering the bottom.
- Beat the egg yolks with the 13 tablespoons of sugar until pale yellow.
- Combine cream and vanilla.
- Heat at medium until almost a boil. Don't let it burn.
- Add the egg yolk mixture and fold in, mixing well. Stir until thickened.
- Cool before pouring over raspberries.
- Sprinkle the raw sugar over the top. I use a small kitchen torch to caramelize it.
- Cool until set, about 1/2 hour.
- Serve with coffee.

*One of the great things about equality is not
just that you be treated equally to a man,
but that you treat yourself equally to the way you treat a man.*

Marlo Thomas

Suzi Battle

Decatur, GA

*If you want a place in
the sun, you've got to
put up with a few blisters.*

Abigail Van Buren

Suzi Battle

First ski experience, Beech
Mountain, NC 1978

Sisters — left to right: Ann, me
and Ellen, Durham, NC 1973

There are many ways to start a biography. The most traditional one starts something like this: "I was born on January 19, 1950 at Watts Hospital in Durham, North Carolina. I was the second of what was to be three girls, no brothers." Or, it could go something like this: "What a life I have had. If you had told me that I would not be rocking babies on the porch of a beautiful home with a white picket fence (and a rose garden), I would not have believed you. Baby, look at me now. A Senior Vice President of a bank, six employees under me, and a six-figure income to boot. What a surprise!"

My life has been a series of surprises…some good, some bad. Some surprises have been joyful, others overwhelmingly sad. There are some decisions I wish I had made differently. But, all in all, the mistakes that I have made have been learning tools, bringing me to the place where I now stand.

- Building a career and the pride that came from achieving something that could be considered a miracle.
- The loves of my life.
- Traveling the world.
- Good food, gardening and music, music, music.

Sad Moments:

- Losing my mother and not really ever knowing her.
- Divorcing.
- The loves of my life who are no longer in my life, whether by my choice or theirs.
- Making mistakes that cannot be undone.

At an Atlanta trade show, 1998

Top of the Eiffel Tower, Paris 1999

Joyful Moments:

- The births of both of my children.
- Being blessed with three wonderful step-children whom I was able to help raise.
- Watching all the children grow into wonderful personalities.
- Creating lasting, loving friendships.
- Time spent with good friends.

Challenges:

- Building a career with no college degree.
- Raising my children as a single parent, after divorcing.
- Fighting the aging body battle.
- Looking for my soul mate.
- Keeping my own identity while trying to build a loving and profound partner-in-life relationship.
- Giving too much to relationships without getting enough back.

Sara's wedding, 1997
First row: daughter Katie, stepdaughter Sara, me, stepdaughter Laura
Back row: son James, stepson Beau

The *Dinner With A Goddess* project has opened up a broader and more loving friendship with the author and her husband. Strong women friends are important, and I have a sense that this project will bring many strong women into my life. It will be an incredible experience to learn about the other 'goddesses' in this book. Of course, the recipes, the art and the poetry will all be a delectable feast.

Suze Battle

Spirituality:

• I have a strong belief in God and in the good that humankind can do on this earth.

• I have always looked for ways to manifest these positive acts, outside the boundaries of the traditional church.

• I am excited about being a patron of a fledgling orphanage in Peru. This feels wonderful.

• I want my children to know what it is to be a great person, doing good deeds.

• I want my children to be kind and learn to be unselfish, while still building their own worth.

At friend's wedding, Stone Mountain, GA 1993

Suzi's Menu

- Wine
- Lemon-Butter Dill Salmon Filets
- Fresh Green Beans
- Wild Rice
- Fresh Baked Oven Rolls
- Lemon Sorbet
- Coffee or Brandy

notes:

Dinner *with* Goddess Suzi

Although I love to cook, my focus at dinner parties is on enjoying my guests. Thus a simple yet elegant meal is imperative. This meal is easy and colorfully pleasing to the eye. Green beans, wild rice and salmon should all be ready at approximately the same time. I have created a meal for a party of six.

Serve with a Chardonnay. I personally prefer the Australians, either Lindemanns or Black Opal.

Wild Rice

Prepare Mahatma wild rice according to directions on the package and then set aside. This rice usually takes 20–25 minutes.

Lemon-Butter Dill Salmon

Ingredients:
- 6 medium salmon filets
- 1 pkg. McCormick's Dip-It Lemon-Butter-Dill Marinade

Method:
- Pre-heat oven to 350°.
- Place salmon filets in an oven browning bag.
- Pour McCormick's Dip-It Lemon-Butter-Dill Marinade into bag.
- Tuck in the end of bag, but do not seal.
- Bake for 20–25 minutes.

notes:

Fresh String Green Beans with Slivered Almonds

Ingredients:
- 1 pound fresh string green beans
- 1 cup slivered almonds, buttered and toasted
- several sprigs of fresh rosemary
- pinch of salt
- 2 tablespoons melted butter

Method:
- Snip off just the ends of the green beans, after washing, and place in a large shallow pan of boiling water.
- Salt beans as needed and mix with fresh rosemary.
- Blanch green beans in uncovered pan for approximately 3–5 minutes, or until just cooked and still crispy.
- Sprinkle with toasted almonds and drizzle butter over the top.

Lemon Sorbet

This is a light and easy dessert that completes my offering. Serve with coffee, wine or brandy.

Life begets life. Energy creates energy.
It is by spending oneself that one becomes rich.

Sara Bernhardt

Vickie Lake

Dunwoody, GA

*True enthusiasm is a fine
feeling whose flash I admire
wherever I see it.*

Charlotte Bronte

Vickie Lake

At grandmother's house,
7 years old, 1964

Feeling good in Florida, 1995

Like most of you, I have developed into quite a different person than imagined in my youth. As a preacher's kid, I saw myself as traditional and looked forward to a predictable future as a homemaker and parent. But life provided many hurdles that altered my path in the most unexpected ways. I still realized my dream of being a homemaker and mother, but I've also had the good fortune of experiencing roles as head of household, entrepreneur, teacher, inventor and am generally a very happy woman.

Getting ready for a workout, Atlanta 1995

I have been able to help hundreds of people regain their own health and vitality through personal instruction. My own experience of feeling so uninformed about my health and physicality lead me to create several products that are now being developed for international distribution. So in a quest for my own healing, I found work that challenges me and helps others. Besides making me feel good, I have been lead to develop a creative side of myself that I would have sworn never existed.

I have lived the cliché that 'your greatest struggles will provide your greatest gifts.' As a child, I had many years of respiratory difficulties that lead to a loss of physical vitality. My efforts to increase my energy (I was living my life and didn't know I was sickly or in pain) channeled my path to a career in fitness. By charting out a unique health system in response to my personal challenges, I developed a program that has enabled me to use a teaching degree, procured in my youth.

This process has also allowed me to raise my child in a manner that I thought I would have to give up as a single parent. When I started my company, I was newly divorced and knew that a career in my degree field would be extremely time consuming. I couldn't imagine that I would have the flexibility or the time with my child that would make us both happy and fulfilled. So, inspired by my love for my son, I started teaching what I truly knew best, how to feel good in one's body.

Soon I had a lucrative business that allowed me to be a full-time mom, even if it meant my son sometimes went to work with me. I was able to create my career exactly the way I wanted. Regarding what I might have been afraid to ask for myself, I had no sense of apology when it came to doing what I thought was best for my child. My experience has been that I never received resistance from my clients, and was usually encouraged and complimented for my commitment. My life experiences have taught me to embrace every obstacle, as each one has opened doors to unimaginable opportunities.

Vickie Lake

Enjoying life, Atlanta, 2002

Cuddling on the couch with Palmer,
Daytona Beach, 1992

With my dear son, Palmer
Atlanta 1989

You can contact Vickie at:
www.thephysicalexperience.com

223

Vickie's Menu

- Fresh Shrimp
  with Three Sauces
- Wine
- Baked Apple Tilapia
- Steamed Broccoli
- Wild Rice Salad
- Strawberry Crêpes

notes:

Dinner with Goddess Vickie

I have always been considered to be a simple cook, missing most of the culinary trappings of gourmet dining. I have typically viewed my commitment to 'clean food' (healthy) and my resistance to experimentation in the kitchen as a personal limitation. But Pamela desired variety in her offering, so here I am publishing one of my healthy recipes. Who would ever have imagined?

The right wines can enhance your meal. Here are some that I prefer: A Montrachet or a Chardonnay is a great choice for the appetizer. A full-bodied oily wine, with oak undertones, holds up well with the hearty shrimp and the spice of the sauces.

The sweet, moderate texture of the Tilapia requires a lighter wine. I typically recommend a light Chardonnay with subtle flavors or a Pouilly Fuissé. I have recently offered Piesporter Goldtropfchen for it's light, crisp texture. I have also been known to 'get away' with a Montrachet, my personal favorite wine. You would definitely not want to choose a sweet wine as it could clash with the flavor of apples in the recipes.

As for dessert, if I were still drinking wine, I would stay with my Montrachet, even though there are many great wines that are created for desserts.

Your locally owned wine store is a great resource. The proprietor is usually a willing and enthusiastic reference for your menu. It is also fun to develop a relationship with your local vendor, who will continue to teach and assist you in your dinner party choices.

The internet is also a great reference for wine purchases. The prices are competitive, the choices are extensive, and information about each wine is abundant. Sometimes it is helpful to be able to read a description, then come back and read it again, before I make my selection. I print out the description of wines as I make purchases, broadening my vocabulary for the textures I enjoy. It also helps me learn which vintages I can trust. I have rarely been disappointed.

Shrimp with Three Sauces

Prepare appetizer items ahead of time. If you are having a casual party, leave the shrimp in the shell, providing a container for discarded shells and a warm cotton cloth for each guest. Thoroughly wet each cloth and roll them individually and place on a plate. Before presenting the towels to your guests, microwave for 15 seconds, or until warm, and top each towel with a wedge of lemon. Be careful since the centers get warmer than the exterior. You don't want a guest with scalded fingers.

Ingredients:
- 36 medium, fresh shrimp
- 2 red peppers sliced
- 2 medium carrots sliced
- 6 stalks of celery sliced

Method:
- Place shrimp into a deep pot with a minimum of 3 quarts boiling water.
- Skim shrimp off the top as they turn pink and float to the surface.
- Place shrimp in the center of a large plate and surround with generous slices of red pepper, carrots, and celery.

Three sauces:

Cocktail Sauce:
- 2/3 cup ketchup
- 2 teaspoons horseradish; add more horseradish for spicier palates
- 1 teaspoon lemon juice

Pomeray Mustard Sauce:
- 1/2 tofu square
- 2 tablespoons Pomeray mustard
- 1 teaspoon small lemon

Tarter Sauce:
- purchase from your local market

notes:

Baked Apple Tilapia

Tilapia is a sweet and moderately hearty fish that is very compatible with the flavor of apples. I particularly enjoy the dichotomy of the sweet fish with a tangy apple. Other apple choices change the flavor of the recipe and are nice for variety. Granny Smiths make for a zingy recipe but can sometimes overwhelm this fresh water fish.

Ingredients:
- 6 pieces of tilapia of equal size
- 1/2 cup of apple juice
- 1/8 section Pink Lady apple, per piece of fish
- 1/8 Vidalia onion, julienned 3 inches in length per piece of fish
- 1/4 cup whole, fresh cilantro leaf
- 1 fresh lime
- 6 pieces parchment or parchment style cooking paper, 7"x 10"
- 6 tin foil, 12"x12"

notes:

notes:

Method:
- Pre-heat oven to 350°.
- Marinate tilapia in apple juice for 15 minutes in a glass dish. (Longer begins to break down the texture of the fish.)
- Place each fish in the center of a piece of aluminum foil that has been lined with parchment.
- Sprinkle with julienne onion and yellow pepper (6-8 short pieces of each), and cilantro leaves, rubbing the leaves between your fingers lightly to release the flavor.
- Squeeze 1/8 piece of lime over fish.
- Lay four thin apple slices, with skin, across the top of the fish.
- Lift the sides of the aluminum foil and fold it down once to close the parchment. Seal the sides of tin foil together and then crimp from the top to the sides in an arch, creating easy handle.
- Bake for 20 minutes or until flaky.
- Open each foil pouch and lift the fish in one piece using a pancake spatula to keep the fish from breaking apart. Place the fish on a warm plate. Gently slip each piece of apple off the fish with a fork, revealing the toppings underneath, and decoratively lay alongside the fish.

Steamed Broccoli

Steam 4-inch stems with flowers of Broccoli, so that they are still slightly firm. You will need 3 or 4 pieces per person. Garnish with a lemon wedge, either on the plate or on the table.

Wild Rice Salad

Ingredients:
- 1 cup wild and brown rice
- 2 tablespoons light tasting olive oil
- 1 tablespoons of chopped golden raisins or dried cranberries
- 2 tablespoons Vidalia onion, finely diced
- 1/4 yellow pepper, finely diced
- 2 teaspoons slivered almonds
- dash of garlic powder
- salt and pepper
- 1/3 Pink Lady apple, coarsely grated
- 1/2 small lemon

Method:
- Cook rice as directed on pkg.
- Squeeze lemon over top.
- Add all other ingredients and toss.
- Serve immediatel, or refridgerate and serve cold.

Strawberry Crêpes with Whipped Cream

I recommend preparing the strawberries and crêpes the day before your dinner. Since you will have already done the preliminaries for your dessert, it's fun to invite your guests into the kitchen while you finish the preparation. Have fun with this presentation. Your personality can really come out here. While you are preparing each plate, you can serve aromatic coffee or open a dessert wine.

Strawberries

Slice 1 pound of strawberries into a ceramic bowl and sweeten with 3-5 drops or 1/4 to 1/2 packet of Stevia. Cover tightly and refrigerate until needed. Save 6 of the best strawberries for garnish.

notes:

Crêpes: 2 per guest

Ingredients:
- 3/4 cup plain flour
- 6 egg whites
- 2 1/2 cups soy or plain milk
- Pinch salt
- 4 to 6 drops or 1/4 to 1/2 packet of Stevia

Method:
- Combine flour, eggs and sugar in a medium mixing bowl.
- Stir flour and milk in alternately, with a wire whisk until smooth. Whip for an additional 60 seconds.
- Refrigerate for at least one hour.
- When you are ready to create the crêpes, the consistency of your batter should be like heavy cream. If your batter thickens, you can thin it with a little water or milk.
- Heat a 6–8 inch, non-stick and slope-sided pan until a sprinkle of water sizzles.
- Place 2–4 tablespoons of batter (depending on the size you want to serve) into the pan and immediately swirl it to thinly cover the surface.
- Cook the crêpes for up to 30 seconds or until the edges brown slightly, or until the surface loses it's wet look. If your batter is thick in the center, you may need to flip the crêpes in the pan for a few seconds to completely cook it.
- Stack the crêpes, separated by a small piece of wax paper.
- Refrigerate up to 2 days, tightly sealed.
- Remove your crêpes when you start preparing dinner so that they are at room temperature when they are filled and served.

Whipped Cream

Ingredients:
- 1 pint heavy whipping cream
- stevia, 1/4 to 1/2 packet

Method:
- As you go into dinner, put the cream container and wire whisk into a ceramic bowl and place in the refrigerator. The similar cool temperature will ensure perfect texture.
- Hand whip the cream, adding 1/4 to 1/2 packet of Stevia immediately before serving.

notes:

Splayed Strawberries

Ingredients:
- 6 saved strawberries

Method:
- Hold a fresh strawberry by the stem and cut narrow slices across the berry.
- Fan the slices, carefully maintaining the stem. I always separate the best berries when I am making my filling.
  These decorative berries stay fresher and present better if they are stored in a small paper bag, as opposed to plastic wrap.

Crêpe Presentation Method:
- Have all your ingredients: prepared crêpes and strawberries, whip cream, and splayed strawberry garnish.
- Individually place 2 tablespoons of strawberry filling into the center of each crêpe, spreading it along the full length of the crepe.
- Fold one end over the filling and then overlap the other end.
- Lift the crêpe and roll it onto a plate with the smooth side up.
- Put two crêpes on each plate and top with a dollop of whip cream and a splayed strawberry.
- If you elect to forego the whipped cream, you can drizzle a small amount of straw berry juice or chocolate syrup over the top of each crêpe. Or swirl the strawberry juice or chocolate syrup in the plate before you lay the filled crêpes on the plate, placing a splayed fresh strawberry between the crêpes.

I Am Woven

Sometimes I am woven
Into a safe soft still luminous cocoon
Made of moonbeams and loon feathers.

Other times I think I am the only weaver
Of sacred cloth for a hundred miles,
And I can't stop my shuttle.

But more and more now I remember
The sweet weaving around me
As I sit or lie dreaming.

Angels and old grandmothers weave me,
Wrap me, then hold me in a warm nest
When I close down my loom and rest.

Mary Feagan

Healing Herbal Teas

For most of history,
Anonymous was a woman.

Virginia Wolf

Healing Herbs *from our* Kitchens

You may be pleasantly surprised to discover that many of the fresh and dried herbs in your kitchen have healing qualities. When most folks think of healing or medicinal herbs, what comes to mind are tinctures or capsules purchased from a local health food store. Before there were tinctures, or capsules, or brightly packaged herbal tea blends, women went to their gardens, opened their kitchen cabinets, or headed down to their root cellars, gathering herbs they needed for both flavoring their food and treating a variety of minor ailments.

What I'm offering is the ritual of preparing and drinking herbal teas, healing the soul as well as the body. For instance, when our bodies drink a cup of mint tea, we receive a nutritionally significant dose of minerals, as well as sinus-clearing menthol. Additionally, our soul is fed by the very act of caring for ourselves and others. Just taking the time to sit and savor the mint taste and aroma nourishes us. Herbal teas can be quite useful in treating common problems such as indigestion, colds and headaches. Other kitchen herbs are also safe and gentle.

1. Herbs found in our kitchens are best used as infusions, or herbal teas. Here's an ideal method for leaves, flowers and seeds when creating your own herbal teas.

Measurements: Use 1 heaping teaspoon of dried herb, or 2-1/2 heaping teaspoons of fresh herb to 1 glass (8 ounce) of water.

Procedure: Put the herb in a pot with a close-fitting lid. Pour freshly boiled water over the herb, put on the lid and let stand for 10 to 20 minutes—then strain. If using your herbal tea for healing, the standard adult dosage is 1/2 cup, three times daily. When using bark or roots, gently simmer the herb for 20 minutes to release the medicinal properties. Make a fresh healing brew daily.

2. Herbal tea strengths for children are different. Children less than seven years old should not be given healing brews without first consulting your health care practitioner. For children seven years and older and for folks over 60 in poor health, start with 1/5th the adult dose. Children 7 to 8 years old can take 2/5ths the adult dose, if no allergic reactions happen. Children nine to ten = 1/2 adult dose; 11 to 12 = 3/5 dose; 13 to 14 = 4/5 dose; 15 and over = full dose, but only after trying a smaller dose. Older adults can gradually work up to a full dose, if no side effects manifest.

3. Herbal self-care is for minor ailments only. Herbs can be useful for more serious acute and chronic diseases, but only under the auspices of a health care practitioner. Anything really serious or life threatening is beyond the scope of this offering. Make sure you have the correct herb, especially if you are growing them yourself. Use only the part of the herb listed. Do not substitute roots for leaves. Check the contraindications for an herb, especially if you are pregnant, nursing or taking medications. If in doubt, consult your doctor or other health care practitioner.

Anise Seed

Good for digestion and respiratory problems, including sinusitis. Promotes milk production in nursing mothers. Can be helpful in alleviating peri-menopausal symptoms.

Basil Leaf

Has fever reducing and antiviral properties that make it useful for dealing with feverish colds and flu. It's also a mild antispasmodic that will help relieve stomach and menstrual cramps, indigestion, constipation and headaches.

Caraway Seed

A calming herb that has the same uses as dill; also stimulates the appetite, helps treat diarrhea and is good for bronchitis.

Cardamom Seed

Good for asthma, bronchitis, colds, flue and digestion, especially with flatulence.

Cayenne Pepper

Use a small amount for indigestion, poor circulation, bleeding ulcers, arthritis and the onset of colds, flu, sore throat and sinus infection. It's good for pain relief when used externally. Avoid contact with eyes.

Celery Seed

Helps improve appetite, relieve muscle spasms, reduce blood pressure; and is helpful for arthritis, gout and stress. Do not use when pregnant

Cinnamon Bark

Warms the body, enhancing digestion, peripheral circulation (cold hands and feet) and meta-bolism of fats. Good for stomach cramps, headaches, nausea, motion sickness, diarrhea, yeast infection, athlete's foot, heavy period and congestion. Do not use large amounts when pregnant.

Coriander Seed

Since it helps with digestion and absorption, it's useful for stomach and intestinal problems. Also, this is an excellent herb for urinary tract tonification and mild cases of cystitis.

Dill Weed and Seed

This is a great remedy for children's colicky stomachaches. Good for adult stomach upset and insomnia caused by indigestion. It will also increase milk flow in nursing mothers.

Fennel Seed

Relieves all forms of digestive distress, cramps, gas, indigestion, constipation, and acid stomach. Has been used as an appetite suppressant, as eyewash and to clear the lungs of congestion. A good all-around tonic, it may also be helpful in alleviating peri-menopausal symptoms.

Fenugreek Seed

Reduces mucus, helping asthma and sinus problems. Good for constipation, fever, eye strain and inflammation. Also promotes lactation in nursing mothers.

Garlic Bulb

This workhorse of the herb world helps both in enhancing the immune function and assisting in detoxification. It is useful in treating abscesses, anal itch (suppository), asthma, athlete's foot, bronchitis, colds and flu, earache, fever, sore throat, infections in general, vaginal discharge, circulatory problems, digestive upset and ulcers. Garlic is not recommended if you are taking anti-coagulants.

Ginger Rhizome

Assists the body in dealing with asthma, bronchitis, colds and flu, digestive upset and cramps, earache, early low-grade fevers, headache (hot foot bath and cold towel on neck), hemorrhoids, delayed periods, motion sickness, morning sickness and nausea, sore throat, circulatory problems, muscle pain and vomiting. Good in the bath for arthritis pain. Too much of a good thing can upset the stomach. Ginger is not recommended for folks on anti-coagulants or if one has gallstones. If pregnant, use sparingly.

Mint

Helps lower fever. Good for relieving colds and flu, indigestion headaches (especially combined with Rosemary leaf), motion sickness and nausea, sore throat, colic, diarrhea and poor appetite. Do not use if you are a nursing mother.

Mustard Seeds

Digestive aid. Can also be applied externally as a plaster for chest congestion, injuries or joint pain. Do not use on children less than age seven. Here's how to make a mustard plaster: Stir one tablespoon of mustard seed powder in a quart of warm water and saturate a towel in this liquid. Rub olive oil over the body area, apply saturated towel, and then cover with plastic first, following with a towel or blanket for approximately 20 minutes.

Oregano Leaf

Herbal immune booster that is effective against bacterial, viral and fungal infection. The best form is the wild oregano—*origanum vulgare*—which is useful in dealing with animal bites, acne, athlete's foot, bee stings, all respiratory problems, diarrhea, gum disease, headaches, muscle pain, gland problems, mild urinary tract infections, and wounds.

Parsley Leaf

Good for digestion and bad breath, bed wetting, fluid retention and flatulence. Huge amounts may stress the liver.

Rosemary Leaf (Needle)

A good herbal antiseptic against bacteria and fungi, stimulates circulation and digestion, helps fight colds and flue, headaches, delayed periods and menstrual cramps. Useful for sore throats as a gargle. Do not use if pregnant.

Sage Leaf

Stimulates the nervous system, good for hot flashes (is a phyto or plant estrogen) and other peri-menopausal symptoms, menstrual cramps, infections of the mouth and throat and to dry up milk when a woman wishes to stop nursing. Used in a foot bath to treat athlete's foot. Do not take if you are epileptic or iron deficient (anemic). Do not use if you are pregnant or breastfeeding.

Thyme Leaf

A strong herbal antiseptic that is effective for sore throats, colds and flu, bronchitis, fever, headache and itchy scalp.

Turmeric Rhizome

An herbal anti-inflammatory that aids circulation, protects the liver and is useful in treating arthritis. Stimulates bile secretion so do not use it if you have bilary tract obstruction. Externally, it is good for bruises and rheumatic pain.

Menu of Recipes

Appetizers

Brie Baskets with Mango (Claude) 44

Bruschetta (Kathy) 93

Crab Appetizer with Crackers (Maggie) 124

Eggplant Appetizer with Pita Bread (Lee) 113

Hommus with Crackers & Pita Bread (Lea) 103

Hommus with Tandoori Nan (Debbie) 53

Hommus with Toasted Pita Wedges (Jill) 81

Melon wrapped with Proscuitto (Mary Ann) 136

Olive Pâté with Warm Bread (Sharon) 207

Shrimp with Three Sauces (Vickie) 225

Spinach & Artichoke Puff Pastry (Garland) 63

Tuna Antipasto (Pola) 165

Veggies in Purple Cabbage Bowl (Annabelle) 25

Salads

Avocado & Tomato Salad (Mary Kay) 147

Baby Bib & Basil Salad (Pamela) 155

'Beautiful' Salad (Kathy) 93

Chickpea Salad (Pola) 166

Green Pea Salad (Garland) 64

Green & Orange Salad (Maggie) 124

Herb & Flower Salad (Cathy) 36

Mixed Baby Greens Salads (Mary Ann) 136

Spinach Salad with Fried Tofu
    & Thai Peanut Sauce Dressing (Debbie) 54

Strawberries & Feta Salad (Sandra) 196

Tabbouleh Salad (Jill) 84

Wild Rice Salad (Vickie) 227

Vinaigrette Dressing (Lee) 113

Soups

Seafood Bisque (Annabelle) 25

Seafood Bisque (Rozelle) 175

White Gazpacho (Mary Kay) 146

Vegetables

Asparagus, baked (Sandra) 197

Asparagus, sautéed (Pamela) 156

Candied Sweet Potatoes (Garland) 64

Deviled Carrots (Rozelle) 177

Green Beans Almondine, Microwave (Garland) 64

Green Beans Almondine, Sautéed (Suzi) 217

Green Bean Bundles (Maggie) 125

Julienne Vegetables (Claude) 45

Popeye's Creamed Spinach (Sally) 187

Roasted Peppers (Pola) 166

Rice Casserole (Sandra) 197

Rice, Saffron Pilaf (Lea) 105

Rice, Mahatma Brown (Pamela) 156

Swiss Chard (Mary Ann) 136

Beef Entrées

Beef Tenderloin
    w/Green Peppercorn Sauce (Claude) 44

Beef Tenderloin
    w/Marinade for Grilling (Maggie) 125

Beef (Ground) with Rice & Yogurt (Jill) 83

Cape Malay Bobotie (Ground Beef) (Rozelle) 176

Manzo Vapore (Pot Roast) (Mary Ann) 137

Menu of Recipes

Chicken Entrées

Chicken Divan (Mary Kay) 146
Chicken Parmesan (Kathy) 95
Chicken Pillows (Garland) 63
Farewell Chicken (Annabelle) 26
Mushroom Chicken Casserole (Jean) 73
Soy Lemon Chicken (Jill) 85

Seafood Entrées

Apple Tilapia (Vickie) 226
Grouper with Garlic Cilantro Sauce (Lea) 104
Heavenly Halibut (Sally) 186
Salmon Supreme (Pamela) 155
Salmon with Lemon/Dill Marinade (Suzi) 217
Salmon with Soy (Sandra) 196
Seafood Pasta (Pola) 167
Spicy Fish Stew (Sharon) 208
Shrimp, New Orleans Style (Lee) 114

Vegetarian Entrées

Fried Tofu on Spinach Salad with Thai Peanut
    Sauce Dressing (Debbie) 54
Gorgonzola Penne Pasta (Sharon) 208
Italian Tomato Sauce, Amy's (Kathy) 94
Wild Asparagus Frittata (Cathy) 35
Yogurt (Jill) 82
Yogurt Cheese (Jill) 83

Pasta

Linguine with Artichokes & Clam Sauce (Lee) 115
Penne Pasta with Gorgonzola Sauce (Sharon) 208
Seafood Pasta (Pola) 167

Breads

Dipping Sauce (Kathy) 93
Wild Fruit Bread (Cathy) 35

Beverages

Herbal Teas (Cathy) 37

Desserts

Almond Biscotti with Vanilla Ice Cream (Kathy) 95
Apple Pie, Mom's 'Best Ever' (Maggie) 127
Baklava (Lea) 105
Bananas Foster (Debbie) 55
Blueberry Bavarian Pie (Garland) 65
Chocolate Mousse Pie (Lee) 115
Crème Brulé (Sharon) 209
Fruit Pizza (Annabelle) 27
Ice Cream Sandwich Layered Cake (Jean) 73
Italian Custard (Mary Ann) 137
Jell-O with Fruit (Sally) 187
Lemon Meringue Pie (Sandra) 199
Mango Mousse (Claude) 45
Peaches & Cream Cheesecake (Annabelle) 27
Pie Crust, double (Maggie) 126
Pie Crust, single (Sandra) 198
Pie Crust, Graham Cracker (Sally) 187
Raspberry Sorbet with Berries
    & Chocolate Sauce (Mary Kay) 147
Rum Cake (Pamela) 157
Strawberry Crêpes
    with Whipped Cream (Vickie) 228
Tipsy Trifle (Rozelle) 177
Tiramisu (Pola) 167
Yogurt Cream Cheese Pie (Sally) 187

It's My Life!

In this moment I engage you, As my True Authentic Self.
I speak my truth to you, As my True Authentic Self
I shine with all the glory, Of my True Authentic Self.
I embrace all the beauty, Of my True Authentic Self.

Chorus:

It's my life, I'm in the flow, it's my life!
It's my life, I have control, it's my life!

I stand in my power, In my power of love.
I move with my power, With my power of love.
I share my power, My power of love.
I grow in my power, In my power of love.

Chorus:

It's my life, I'm in the flow, it's my life!
It's my life, I have control, it's my life!

I live my life fully, With truth and dignity.
I live my life fully, With great integrity.
I live my life fully, I live it honestly.
I live my life fully, Plugged into unity.

Chorus:

It's my life, I'm in the flow, it's my life!
It's my life, I have control, it's my life!

Release:

I am open to receive, all the possibilities.
I am open to receive, all the possibilities.

©Colleen Campbell, Songwriter, 2001

What If

What if we chose to turn the other cheek?
What kind of message would that send?

What if we expressed our intolerance for these acts by attending to each
other's needs, giving none of our precious energy to our attackers?

What if we chose to respond with love,
out of respect for our selves and those who perished?

What if we chose to forgive our selves and each other?

What if we truly believed that love conquers all?

What if so many of us around the globe sent out so much
love and, so many high vibration, intentions that further terrorists
plans of action were rendered powerless, impotent and unsatisfying?

What if we truly believed we have the power
within us to accomplish that shift in consciousness?

What if we could 'truly say and feel we are one'?
What would be required to bring that about?

What if each of us, just contemplating alternative options and actions,
began a snowball affect that ultimately facilitated the development
of a new diplomacy and conflict resolution methods?

What if we all started right now.

Kathleen Doherty • After 9-11-01

Personal Prayer

I ask for support from all in the Universe

who are aligned with me in consciousness,

All the Beings of Light who form the

Embodiment of Divine Consciousness,

To assist me in balancing and aligning

my humanity with my Divinity

so I may truly say and feel,

We Are One.

Pamela Daniele • April 1986